lonely planet

POCKET CHARLESTON & SAVANNAH

Amy C Balfour

Contents

Top: Bonaventure Cemetery (p146)
Bottom: Savannah Historic District (p115)

Plan Your Trip 4

Mount Pleasant Waterfront Park (p92)

★ Top Experiences

The Journey Begins Here

If you think you know Charleston and Savannah, think again. Their charisma remains undeniable, from the pastel insouciance of Rainbow Row to the live-oak splendor of Forsyth Park. But change is afoot, and the cities thrum with a creative energy that's downright addictive. Just ignore the traffic. A new museum in Charleston re-examines the past while celebrating the present, and the Savannah riverfront boasts a whole new look...and, well, a dinosaur. New rooftop bars overlook church steeples and cargo ships, while creative districts welcome entrepreneurs and restaurateurs. As always, salt marshes and sandy beaches await exploration in the Lowcountry.

Amy C Balfour
@amycbalfour
Amy is a writer and guidebook author covering food, travel and adventure.

Folly Beach (p94)
DANIELA DUNCAN/GETTY IMAGES ©

THE BEST

Outdoor Experiences

Graceful bridges swoop over shimmering salt marshes in the Lowcountry, providing a gorgeous backdrop. But outdoor enthusiasts know these pretty spans are also portals to outdoor fun, from kayaking and motorboating to beachcombing and bird-watching.

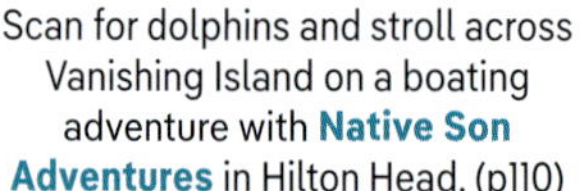

Scan for dolphins and stroll across Vanishing Island on a boating adventure with **Native Son Adventures** in Hilton Head. (p110)

Walk to the center of the **Arthur J Ravenel Bridge** (pictured left) for a beautiful – if windy – sunset with views across the Cooper River. (p92)

Enjoy a leisurely paddle through the salt marshes off **Kiawah Island** and look for herons, eagles and barrier island wildlife. (p94)

Bounce around **Daufuskie Island** (pictured right) on a golf cart, pausing for historic schools and pond-side cocktails. (p106)

Pitch your tent under palm trees beside the beach on **Hunting Island** and sleep under the sea breeze. (p109)

Birdwatchers, grab your binoculars to scope out the shorebirds and songbirds along trails at **Fort Pulaski National Monument**. (p156)

Right: Kiawah Island (p94)

THE BEST

History Experiences

Important players in their country's story, Charleston and Savannah have long worn their history on their 18th-century sleeves. However, moving with the times, museums and plantations today give voice to a wide range of people.

Immerse yourself in exhibits exploring the African American diaspora in the US at the **International African American Museum**. (pictured left; p52)

Tour the **McLeod Plantation**, a cotton plantation whose story encapsulates a larger one about slavery and emancipation in the South. (p86)

See where the Civil War began after a ferry ride to **Fort Sumter**. (pictured right; p58)

Learn about the Reconstruction Era after the Civil War at three separate sites in **Beaufort and the surrounding sea islands**. (p102)

Imagine the chatter of oyster shuckers – you'll swear you can almost hear them – while exploring the old factory at **Pin Point Heritage Museum**. (p154)

Right: McLeod Plantation (p86)

THE BEST

Beach Experiences

Charleston is surrounded by barrier islands with wide sandy beaches. A short drive from downtown will have you sunbathing, swimming and beachcombing along the Atlantic Ocean in no time. Savannah locals make the short trip to Tybee Island for sun and sand.

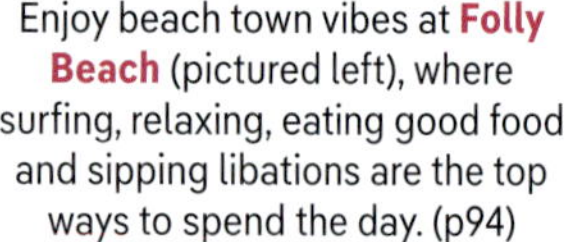

Enjoy beach town vibes at **Folly Beach** (pictured left), where surfing, relaxing, eating good food and sipping libations are the top ways to spend the day. (p94)

Sunbathe on spacious **North Beach** on Tybee Island, then walk north to watch the container ships. (p156)

Drive onto posh Kiawah Island to spend a day at the gorgeous **Kiawah Beachwater Park** (pictured right), where you can also ride a bike on the sand. (p94)

Spend the morning on the beach, then visit the nature center and climb the lighthouse at **Hunting Island State Park** near Beaufort. (p108)

For a few hours of decompression, drop your chair on the sand at **Sullivan's Island** south of Mount Pleasant – no commercial activities permitted here. (p94)

Right: Tybee Island (p157)

THE BEST

Spooky Experiences

Charleston and Savannah are considered to be among the most haunted cities in America, and for good reason. The cities histories' are inextricably tied to slavery and the Confederacy, and countless battles were fought nearby.

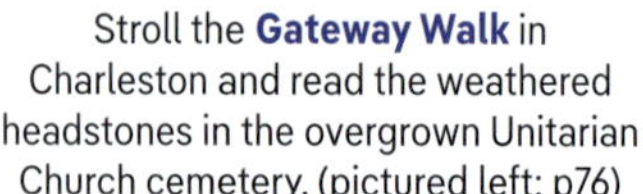

Stroll the **Gateway Walk** in Charleston and read the weathered headstones in the overgrown Unitarian Church cemetery. (pictured left; p76)

In Charleston, join an eerie night walk with **Bulldog Tours**, stopping at the Old City Jail (pictured right), the Provost Dungeon or the city's oldest graveyard. (p46)

Spend an hour walking past statues and headstones under the shade of moss-draped live oaks at **Bonaventure Cemetery** in Savannah. (p146)

Learn the facts behind some of Savannah's most macabre stories on an evening walk with **True History Tours**. (p128)

Take a tour of the **Mercer-Williams House**, the site of Savannah's most famous murder. (p126)

Right: Bonaventure Cemetery (p146)

THE BEST

Lowcountry Experiences

Fresh seafood and sun-kissed views of marshes and beaches are perpetual draws, but the ongoing efforts of the Gullah-Geechee to preserve their culture anchor the region's story and underscore the need to protect this special landscape.

Peel shrimp and eat oysters while soaking up the sunset beside the marsh at **Bowens Island Restaurant**, the best seafood shack around. (p94)

Admire Lowcountry classics – an oak alley, a boneyard beach, tabby ruins and sweeping marshland – on a drive through **Botany Bay** (pictured left; p90).

Learn the unique history of a longstanding sea island community on a tour with **Gullah-N-Geechee Mahn Tours**. (p108)

Walk the 1.5-mile Avenue of Oaks at **Wormsloe Historic Site**, flanked by hundreds of live oaks, then learn the history of the plantation. (p150)

Shop for the perfect sweetgrass basket beside the **Mount Pleasant Visitor Center** (p92) in Mount Pleasant or at the **Four Corners of Law** (pictured right; p43).

Right: Wormsloe State Historic Site (p150)

1733 WORMSLOE 1913

THE BEST

Art Experiences

The Savannah College of Art & Design (SCAD) fuels the vibrant scene in Savannah, dubbed the Creative Coast. Earning kudos for its galleries and museums, Charleston hosts a delightful art walk on the third Thursday of the month.

Pay your respects to the famous Bird Girl, then appreciate the beauty of the rotunda and its grand canvases at Savannah's **Telfair Academy**. (pictured left; p126)

Peruse the always compelling temporary exhibits at the **Jepson Center** in Savannah to see what's new, then grab lunch at its airy cafe. (pictured right; p126)

Chat with locals about art on a late-afternoon stroll past murals, bright storefronts and a range of galleries in Starland during Savannah's **First Friday art walk**. (p138)

Mimic the poses of the Lowcountry's fanciest forebears, whose likenesses gaze out from stately portraits in Charleston's **Gibbes Museum**. (p76)

Be surprised at the **SCAD Museum of Art**, with 4500 works in its impressive collection. (p128)

Right: SCAD Museum of Art (p128)

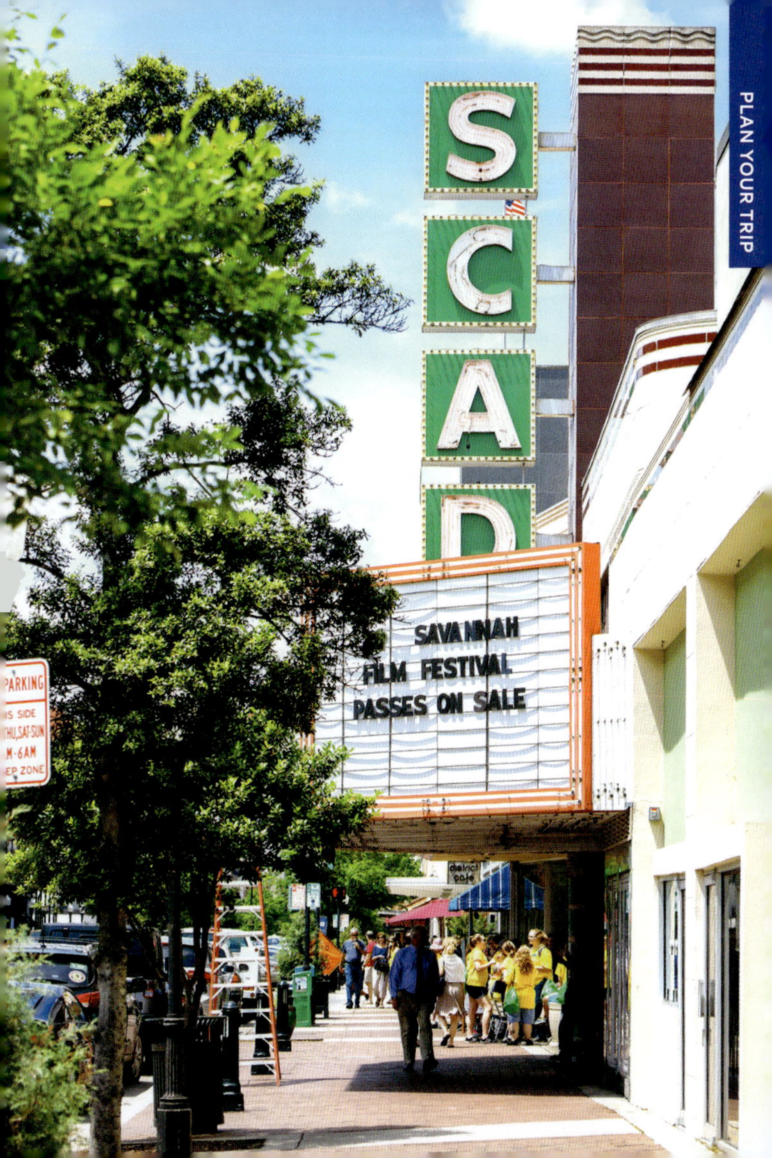
SCAD
SAVANNAH
FILM FESTIVAL
PASSES ON SALE
PARKING

JAMES ZURAW/THE REFINERY ©

The Refinery (p66)

THE BEST

Nightlife Experiences

Balmy Charleston evenings are perfect for sipping craft cocktails or dancing to live jazz. Savannah's revelers take advantage of open-container regulations, bouncing between downtown waterholes along rollicking nightlife corridors. Both cities have excellent rooftop patios.

Sip a cocktail and survey the beauty of Charleston under moonlight at the **Citrus Club**, atop the Dewberry Hotel. (p66)

Listen to live music with river breezes keeping things cool at **The Refinery** or one of Charleston's many outdoor music venues. (p66)

Sing crowd-selected favorites off rowdy River St at **Savannah Smiles Dueling Pianos**. (p129)

Bust out your best moves to indie, rock, soul and funk bands at Savannah's hip **El-Rocko Lounge**. (p131)

Appreciate a well-crafted drink in cozy underground digs that hearken back to an earlier time at **Alley Cat Lounge** in Savannah's Historic District. (p131)

Best for Kids

Spend a rainy day in Charleston at the **South Carolina Aquarium**, where kids adore the touch tank and the sea turtle rehab center. (p64)

Let the kids loose at **Isle of Palms County Park**, which has a playground. The swimming area is monitored seasonally by lifeguards. (p93)

Walk along the riverfront in Savannah to see the cargo ships and cool off at the **Plant Riverside** splash pad. (p121)

Step into immersive works of art at the **Children's Art Museum** inside the Jepson Center in Savannah. (p129)

Get goosebumps during **spooky tours** in the **Charleston** (p46) and **Savannah** (p148) historic districts.

Best for Free

Search for the statue of 'Little Gracie' and soak up the Southern Gothic vibe at Savannah's atmospheric **Bonaventure Cemetery**. (p146)

Walk the trails and gardens and learn about the Lowcountry at the **Coastal Discovery Museum** in Hilton Head. (p109)

Walk down Bull St in Savannah to admire the **city squares**, which are marked by monuments and Spanish-moss-draped live oaks. (p124)

There's plenty of free street parking – keep all wheels off the road – close to the distraction-free beauty of the **beach on Sullivan's Island**. (p94)

Watch Citadel students march across their parade grounds during a **full dress parade** on Friday afternoon in Charleston. (p64)

Perfect Days

Let buttermilk biscuits and cheese grits fuel your adventures through historic cityscapes and the languid beauty of the Lowcountry. Swing by a white-sand beach and end with seafood in the evening.

DAY ONE

Only Have One Day?

MORNING

Meander around Charleston's awe-inspiring **Historic District** (p42) or join a tour with **Charleston Footprints** (p46).

AFTERNOON

Pause for lunch at **Gaulart & Maliclet** (p44) or **Poogan's Porch** (pictured above left; p80), then delve into the new **International African American Museum** (p52). Catch the last tour of the **Nathaniel Russell House** (p44).

EVENING

Feast at **FIG** (p68) or drop into **167 Raw** (p68) (no reservations). After dinner stroll a bit more, popping into and out of any cocktail bar that catches your eye. For a great night view of the city, stop at the rooftop **Pavilion Bar** (p46) or **Citrus Club** (p66).

Nathaniel Russel House

DAY TWO

A Weekend Trip

MORNING

Hit the Ashley River plantations. **Drayton Hall** (p67) is home to America's oldest plantation house, while the **Magnolia Plantation** (p67) has a magnificent swamp trail. **Middleton Place** (p67) has the oldest gardens in the US and they are exquisite.

AFTERNOON

Return to the city for lunch at the **Pass** (p80) or **Xiao Bao Biscuit** (p81), then go craft boozing at **Revelry Brewing Co** (p69) or **Firefly Distillery** (p66).

EVENING

For dinner, stop at Edmunds Oast for fine gastropub fare or enjoy the festive vibe at **Leon's Oyster Shop** (pictured above center; p64). Attend a minor-league game at **'the Joe'** (p65) or try a ghost tour with **Bulldog Tours** (p46).

DAY THREE

A Short Break

MORNING

Soak up Southern charm in the Savannah Historic District. Start at the southern end of **Forsyth Park** (p118) and pause by the monuments and fountain. Amble up Bull St to Monterey Sq and the **Mercer-Williams House** (p126).

AFTERNOON

Take a decadent Southern lunch at **Mrs Wilkes Dining Room** (p130), then walk it off by heading to the **Cathedral Basilica of St John the Baptist** (p127) and the **Telfair Academy** (p126).

EVENING

Dinner is upscale Southern classics at festive Planter's Tavern in the **Olde Pink House** (pictured above right; p130) basement. Catch a **dark history tour** (p128) before cocktails at **Alley Cat Lounge** (p131).

If You Have More Time

For wide beaches and pretty Lowcountry seagrasses, drive to East Savannah & the Islands. Begin the day basking in the sun on **Tybee Island**. Check out the **Lighthouse** (p157) and **North Beach** (p156), then pop into **Fort Pulaski** (p156) on your return to the mainland.

For a casual lunch, stop at **Sisters of the New South** (p159) for a plate of soul food and a slice of red-velvet cake. Drive south and spend the afternoon exploring **Wormsloe Historic Site** (p150) and the nearby **Pin Point Heritage Museum** (p154).

In the evening, settle in for sunset drinks and dinner by the marsh at **Wyld** (p151), then return to River St in Savannah to stroll along the water from bar to bar. End at **Plant Riverside** (p121). Admire the natural history treasures in the lobby, then enjoy a nightcap and great river views on one of the plant's **rooftop bars** (p123).

Tybee Island Lighthouse (p157)

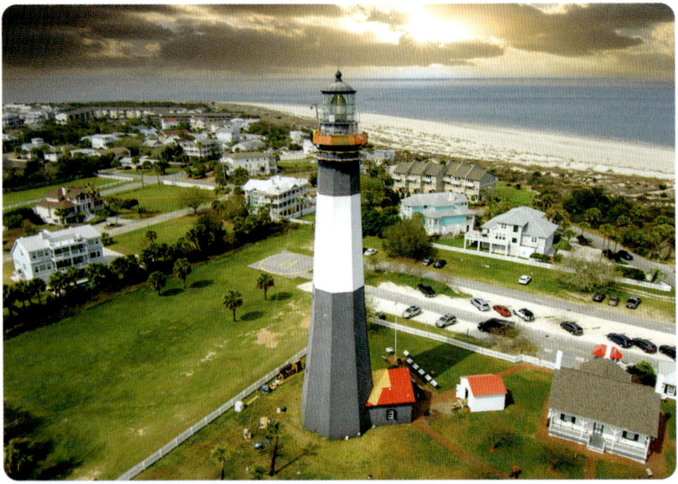

A City Day Trip

A one-hour drive from Savannah lands you in charming Beaufort, which is surrounded by sea islands. Walk past the downtown waterfront and nearby historic homes, then join a **golf cart tour** (p106) spotlighting native son and writer Pat Conroy. Enjoy a delicious lunch at **Lowcountry Produce** (p111), then pick up a map of local sites at the **Reconstruction Era National Historical Park** (p102).

Drive to St Helena Island to poke around the **Penn Center** (p108), a Gullah-Geechee hub. Continue to **Hunting Island State Park** (p108) to hike through a maritime forest. Conclude at **Parris Island**, a Marine Corps training ground with a fascinating **museum** (pictured left; p108) about the corps.

On a Rainy Day

With its many museums and historic-house tours, Charleston is a fun place to spend a rainy day. Exhibits at the **Charleston Museum** (p65) skilfully trace the history of the city. Add on a tour of the nearby **Aiken-Rhett House** (p56). Animal lovers can explore the critter-filled **South Carolina Aquarium** (pictured right; p64).

A rainy day in Savannah is the perfect time to explore all three Telfair Museums: the **Telfair Academy** (p126), the **Jepson Center for the Arts** (p126) and the **Owens-Thomas House**. The many natural history treasures inside the **JW Marriott Plant Riverside** (p121) lobby are also worth a rainy-day gander.

Get Prepared

BOOK AHEAD

Three months before
Make reservations for top hotels and restaurants, particularly in downtown areas.

One month before
Check online listings for upcoming theater, music and comedy performances, especially during peak months.

One week before
Decide on tours and book tickets. Some require a minimum number of people, so secure the right one in advance rather than just showing up.

Manners Matter

Locals ooze Southern charm and politeness. Don't be alarmed when people want to chat to you and learn your life story – and tell you theirs – anywhere you go.

Handshakes are common when meeting men and women for the first time. Say 'hello' and 'goodbye' to staff when visiting shops, restaurants and sights. Queues, known as lines, are dutifully respected.

Parking

Many downtown hotels in Charleston and Savannah offer overnight parking, but for a price. Valet parking runs about $50 per night. Self-parking on hotel grounds in downtown areas is rare. If it's available, expect a fee of $15 to $25 per night.

To save money, check out city-run garages near your hotel. Street parking is also typically free at night (with the exception of a section of King St, Charleston).

Things to Know

You can take booze-filled drinks 'to go' in plastic cups in the Historic District in Savannah, meaning you can saunter through downtown without fear of getting arrested for having an open container.

If you'd like to get out on the water in Charleston but don't have time for the Fort Sumter trip or a guided excursion, hop on the Charleston Water Taxi, which loops across the Cooper River between Mount Pleasant and downtown Charleston. It's $17 for an all-day pass and no reservations are required.

When exploring cemeteries, churches or hallowed grounds, be respectful of the place and of those around you. Keep your voice low and children and pets under control.

TIPPING

Tipping in restaurants with table service is compulsory.

Restaurant

Bar
or 15–20% of total bill

$3–5 per day

Hotel
for housekeeping staff, $1 per bag for porters

Guided tour
for guides/ for drivers

DAILY BUDGET

BUDGET: Less than $200

- Campsite: **from $70**
- Room in budget hotel: **$90–135**
- Taco: **$6**
- Pint of beer: **$7**
- Bicycle rental: **$25–40**

MIDRANGE: $200–350

- Room in midrange hotel: **$150–300**
- Shrimp and grits: **$25**
- Glass of wine: **$11**
- Car rental: **$56–75**

TOP END: More than $350

- High-end accommodation: from **$465**
- Top-flight meals (with tax and tip): **from $125**
- Guided tour: **$40–100**
- Craft cocktail: **$16**

Currency
US dollar ($)

Languages
English, Gullah

Time
Eastern Standard Time (GMT/UTC minus five hours)

PACKING

Pack a bathing suit, particularly if you're visiting in the spring, summer, winter...or fall. Also bring dependable walking shoes. You will likely do a lot of walking – it's the best way to explore these cities.

GEORGE DOLGIKH/SHUTTERSTOCK ©

When to Go

Anytime is a good time to visit Charleston and Savannah, although you won't be hitting the chilly beaches from November through February.

The months of March through May and September through November offer great weather and lots of festivals in Charleston. Summers are hot and muggy, while winters are on the chilly side (it unexpectedly snowed in January 2018). April and October are the two busiest months for tourism in Savannah. That is when the weather is at peak perfection – the heat and humidity either haven't reached oppressive levels yet or have just broken, much to everyone's relief.

The Big Events

February: Charleston kicks off the year with the **Lowcountry Oyster Festival** at Boone Hall Plantation. The **Southeastern Wildlife Expedition (SEWE)** comes to Savannah mid-month. This massive wildlife art event has exhibits, demos and social events. Savannah hosts the **Black Heritage Festival** over three weeks in February, coinciding with Black History Month.

March: The **Charleston Festival** in Charleston is a lovely celebration of architecture, history, gardens and culture, with house and garden tours. Watch the **St Patrick's Day Parade** (p120) in Savannah – it's the second largest St Patrick's Day parade in the world after New York City's.

April/May: The well-attended **Cooper River Bridge Run** in April is a 10km race over the Ravenel Bridge, which links Mount Pleasant to Charleston. In May, the Holy City hosts the performing-arts extravaganza **Spoleto Festival USA**, which takes place over 17 days. It's South Carolina's largest event.

Charleston Weather

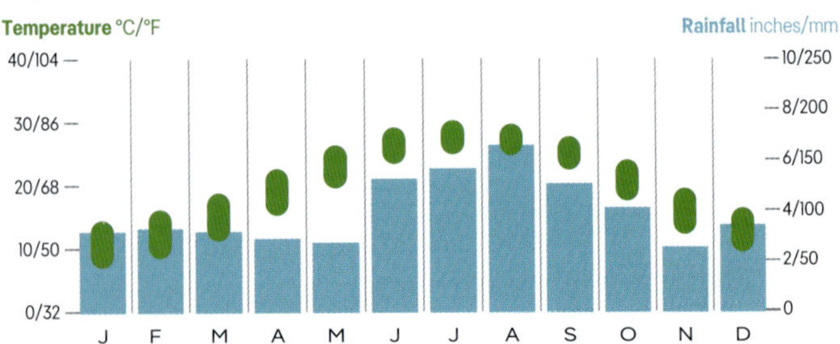

JT BLATTY/ALAMY STOCK PHOTO ©

St Patrick's Day Parade, Savannah

October: Held in the last weekend in September and the first week in October, the **MOJA Arts Festival** includes spirited poetry readings and gospel concerts that mark Charleston's celebration of African American and Caribbean culture.

Niche & Nifty

January: On New Year's Day, bold individuals dress like Bill Murray and jump into the freezing cold water at Folly Beach in Charleston during the **Bill Murray Look-a-Like Polar Plunge** (p95). There's also a contest for the best dressed.

May: Celebrate Lowcountry African American culture with storytelling and music on Memorial Day weekend in Beaufort at the **Original Gullah Festival** (p110).

October: Pirates of all shapes and species flock to Tybee Island for a parade and concerts during the **Pirate Fest** (p157).

November: Dig into challah, potato latkes and NY-style deli sandwiches at the **Shalom Y'all Jewish Food Festival** in Savannah, hosted by Congregation Mickve Israel.

ACCOMMODATIONS LOWDOWN

In Charleston, hotel prices are at their highest during spring break and at Easter. Savannah experiences high-season tourism, and high prices to match, from March through early June, but in the winter months (outside of Christmas) prices plummet.

Getting There

Many travelers arrive in Charleston and Savannah in their own vehicles, but both cities are well connected and easy to access by plane, train and bus.

From the Airport

From Charleston International Airport to Charleston

Transportation pickup is outside the baggage claim area of the terminal.

Bus On CARTA buses, $2 gets you downtown on bus 11 (Dorchester/Airport). Follow the signs for public transportation/CARTA. The airport bus stop is near the passenger pickup area and the rental-car lot. You'll be let off at the intersection of Meeting and Mary Sts near the Charleston Visitor Center.

Car There are eight national rental-car companies at the airport. Pick up your car in the Rental Car Pavilion just past baggage claim at the end of the terminal.

Taxi, rideshare and hotel shuttle Taxis are easy to find outside the terminal. A taxi ride from the airport to downtown typically costs from $40 to $75. For taxis without meters, agree on a rate in advance. Rideshare fares from the airport to downtown Charleston start at $20. You catch the driver outside baggage claim. Some hotels run their own airport shuttles.

From Savannah/Hilton Head International Airport to Savannah

The Savannah/Hilton Head International Airport is about 5 miles west of downtown, off I-95; service is mainly domestic flights to eastern seaboard, Southern and Midwestern cities.

Bus Chatham Area Transit *(CAT; catchacat.org)* offers cheap and convenient transport to and from the airport with its 100X Airport Express route *($8 roundtrip)*. Many hotels, particularly the chains in the vicinity of the airport, offer free shuttles; inquire directly with your hotel for details.

Car There are nine rental-car agencies at the airport. Their offices are located near baggage claim.

Other Points of Entry

Amtrak Stations

Amtrak's daily Silver Service/Palmetto Route links Savannah and Charleston with New York City. The Amtrak station is a few miles west of the Historic District in Savannah. Amtrak also stops at the North Charleston Transit Center, which is also a hub for CARTA.

Getting Around

The historic districts in downtown Charleston and Savannah are easily explored on foot. If you're visiting for a weekend and staying in these areas, you may not need to rent a car. City shuttle buses, pedicabs and rideshares are easily found. However, you will need a car to reach the beaches and sea islands efficiently.

On Foot

Sidewalks link shops, restaurants, churches, museums and historic homes in downtown Charleston. Just be aware that older sidewalks may be a little uneven.

Sidewalks also connect the city's famous town squares in Savannah's Historic District. The wide riverwalk area between River St and the Savannah River is free of cars and well suited to pedestrians.

There's helpful signage at the busiest intersections in both cities.

City Shuttle & Bus

Free DASH buses loop around the Charleston peninsula on three routes. All stop at the visitor center. Use the Green Line to explore the Historic District. CARTA also operates 16 regular bus routes and three express routes. One-way fares for regular/express routes are $2/3.50.

Free hop-on-hop-off DOT shuttles run through downtown Savannah. The Blue Downtown loop runs east–west. The purple Forsyth loop runs north and south around Forsyth Park. Beyond downtown, Chatham Area Transit (CAT) buses are available. Fares start at $1.50.

ESSENTIAL APP

Download the **CARTA Transit app/ CATApp** for information about bus services in Charleston/Savannah.

Bike

With level topography and short city blocks to keep cars from speeding, the Charleston Peninsula is a good place to cycle. There are a handful of bike and e-bike shops in and around downtown. **Lime** (p49; *li.me/locations/charleston*) runs an e-bike-sharing program.

A bike is an efficient way to explore Savannah, and there are a couple of rental shops downtown. A few tour companies explore the city by bike. **Savannah on Wheels**, just west of Forsyth Park, rents bikes and leads tours of the Historic District. Cycling is a fun and easy way to explore Tybee Island. You can also rent a golf cart – it's how Tybee locals get around.

Water Taxi & Ferry

The **Charleston Water Taxi** *(charlestonwatertaxi.com)* loops between four stops on the Cooper River. Destinations on the Charleston Peninsula include Waterfront Park (p92) and the Charleston Maritime Center beside the South Carolina Aquarium (p64). Stops on the Mount Pleasant side are Patriots' Point and the Charleston Harbor Resort and Marina. An all-day pass is $17.

The **Savannah Belles Ferry** *(connectonthedot.com)* is a free and easy way to get out on the water. It travels between Waving Girl Landing on River St and Hutchison Island, home of the Westin Savannah Golf Resort and the Savannah Convention Center.

Parking

Charleston

Parking at city-run garages costs $1 per half hour. City-run parking lots cost $1 to $2 per half hour. There may be discounted flat fees after 5pm. Some lots accept payment through a posted parking app or via pay-by-text. The text option seems to be more efficient. Street parking at meters costs $1 per half hour, and meters accept coins and credit cards. Meters are in operation from 9am to 6pm Monday through Saturday.

Savannah

There are five public garages in downtown Savannah and more than 3000 metered parking spots. Metered spots cost 30¢ to 75¢ per hour. Meters are enforced north of Liberty St from 8am to 8pm Monday through Saturday. South of Liberty St they are enforced from 8am to 5pm Monday through Friday. Rates at public parking garages are $1 for the first hour and 75¢ for each hour or portion of an hour after that. You can download the **ParkSavannah app** to pay by cell phone.

You've also got to pay to park on Tybee Island between 8am and 8pm every day year-round. It's $4 per hour. Pay at the kiosk or download the ParkTYB app to pay by cell phone.

Guided cycling tour, Savannah

JEFFREY GREENBERG/UNIVERSAL IMAGES GROUP VIA GETTY IMAGES ©

TRAVEL COSTS

Bike rental
from $25 per day

Golf-cart rental
$169 per day

Pedicab ride
$10–15 per 10 minutes

USE RIDESHARE

Taxi services can be unreliable in downtown Charleston; Uber and Lyft are best for short trips.

CITY BUS TICKETS

Charleston	**$**
DASH shuttle	free
Fixed route bus one-way	$2
Express route bus one-way	$3.50
Day pass	$7
Savannah	**$**
DOT shuttle	free
One-way bus	$1.50
Day pass	$3
Weekly pass	$14

CHARLESTON DASH ROUTES

Green
Meeting & King Sts

Orange
College of Charleston & SC Aquarium

Purple
King & Broad Sts

A Few Surprises

From Spanish moss to Gullah-Geechee legends to unique architecture, sights in Charleston and Savannah can be charmingly unexpected.

Spanish Moss & Live Oaks

Spanish moss dangles from the branches of live oaks throughout the Lowcountry, though it's not Spanish and it's not moss – it's a flowering plant related to the pineapple known as an epiphyte. Rumor has it that the French came up with the name as a likely insult, implying the tangled strands resembled the beards of Spanish conquistadores.

Haint Blue & Bottle Trees

You'll notice lots of porch ceilings in Charleston and Savannah are painted 'haint' blue, a color thought by the Gullah people to ward off evil *haints* (spirits). It also deters insects.

You'll also likely see a few bottle trees on a drive through the Lowcountry. Look for cobalt-blue glass bottles covering the branches of small trees. According to West African lore – brought to Southern states by the enslaved – the bright bottles captured the attention of curious evil spirits, who would slip inside and get trapped. The next day they'd be destroyed by sunlight.

Charleston Single Houses

Single houses are the basic unit of architecture in downtown Charleston. These long, narrow homes were built in the 18th and 19th centuries and resemble English row houses. Though they can vary in architectural style (and are often Georgian, Federal or Italianate), a traditional single house is always one room wide, two rooms deep and a couple of stories tall. They're oriented perpendicular to the street and have lovely, slanting piazzas facing south or west for drainage and to catch a breeze.

OFFBEAT CHARLESTON & SAVANNAH

Break out your pirate duds for the **Pirate Fest** (p157) on Tybee Island in October.

Figurines and taxidermy keep things quirky inside **Graveface** (p140) record store in Savannah.

It's a battle of the ivories at **Savannah Smiles Dueling Pianos** (p129).

Hunt for the statue of the five rockin'-out cherubs in the **Middleton Place gardens** (p67), outside Charleston.

MAKASANA/GETTY IMAGES ©

Bottle trees

DENTON RUMSEY/SHUTTERSTOCK ©

Single house architecture

Explore Charleston

Charleston's Tours

Angel Oak Tree, Johns Island (p92)
ROBERT LOE/GETTY IMAGES ©

See p47
for eating, drinking and shopping listings

Explore South of Broad & the French Quarter

Whether you stroll along the Battery, poke around a palatial historic home or peer through a wrought-iron gate at a flourishing garden, you'll quickly see that the storybook Southern charm of the peninsula's southeastern tip cannot be exaggerated. South of Broad exudes quiet elegance, and it has long been considered the zenith of Charlestonian prosperity. In the French Quarter, romance and history emanate from cobblestone streets, and the city's oldest buildings perch among tempting restaurants and vibrant galleries. Many top-notch hotels are found here too, and several have rooftop bars with grand views of the city.

Getting around

Walking

South of Broad and the French Quarter are easily navigated on foot, though it's a good idea to watch where you're going because the sidewalks can be uneven.

Bus

A couple of CARTA (p29) bus routes, including the free Meeting/King St DASH shuttle, serve these neighborhoods.

Bicycle

Charleston's bike-share program, Lime's Charleston Spokes (p30), has stations in the area.

Rainbow Row (p44)
FIIPHOTO/SHUTTERSTOCK ©

THE BEST

HISTORIC HOUSE Nathaniel Russell House (p44)

MUSEUM Old Slave Mart Museum (p40)

ROOFTOP BAR Pavilion (p46)

LUNCH DEAL Gaulart & Maliclet (p44)

WATERING HOLE Blind Tiger (p47)

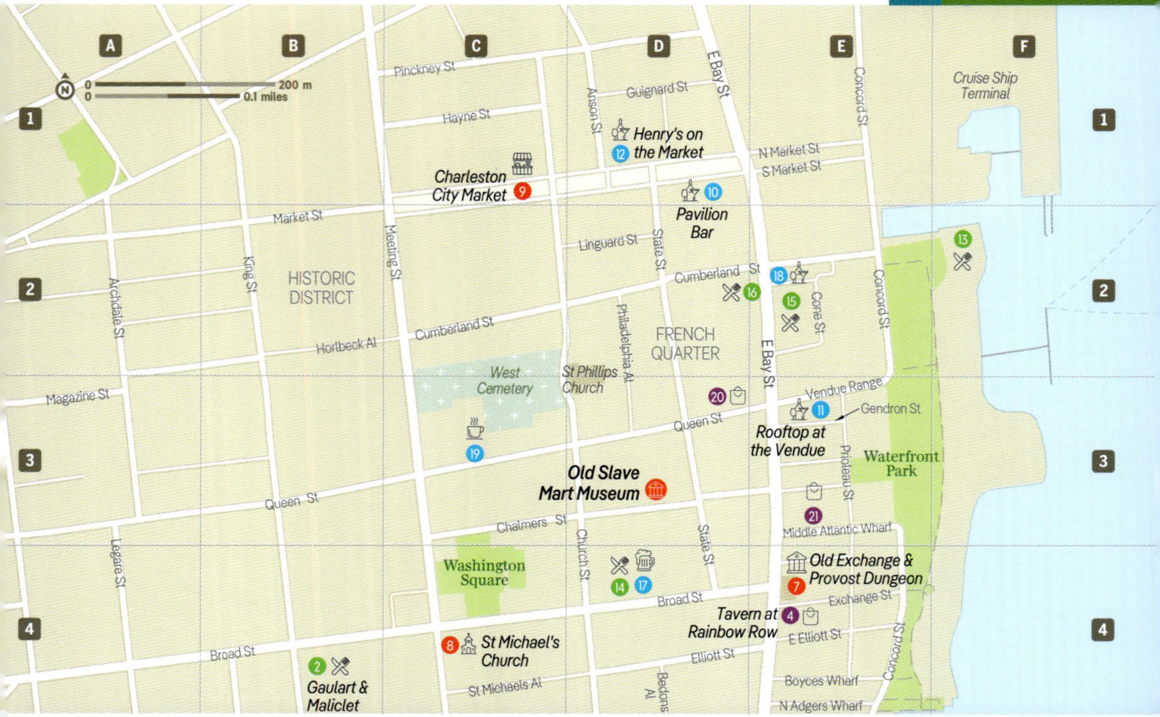

A B C D E F
1 2 3 4
0 200 m
0 0.1 miles
N

Cruise Ship Terminal
Pinckney St
Guignard St
Hayne St
Anson St
E Bay St
Concord St
Henry's on the Market 12
N Market St
S Market St
Charleston City Market 9
Pavilion Bar 10
Market St
Linguard St
State St
Cumberland St
18
16
15
Cone St
13
King St
HISTORIC DISTRICT
Archdale St
Meeting St
Cumberland St
Hortbeck Al
Philadelphia Al
FRENCH QUARTER
West Cemetery
St Phillips Church
20
Vendue Range
Gendron St
11
Rooftop at the Vendue
Magazine St
19
Queen St
Prioleau St
Waterfront Park
Old Slave Mart Museum
Queen St
Chalmers St
21
Middle Atlantic Wharf
Church St
State St
Washington Square
14 17
Old Exchange & Provost Dungeon 7
Legare St
Broad St
Exchange St
Tavern at Rainbow Row 4
E Elliott St
Broad St
8 St Michael's Church
Elliott St
2 Gaulart & Maliclet
St Michaels Al
Bedons Al
Boyces Wharf
N Adgers Wharf
Concord St

For more see
Top Experiences p40
Experiences p44
Eating p47
Drinking p47
Shopping p47
Heyward-Washington House 1
Rainbow Row 3
Nathaniel Russell House 5
Battery & White Point Garden 6
SOUTH OF BROAD
Charleston Harbor
Cooper River
Ashley River
E Bay St
S Adgers Wharf
Longitude La
Stoll's Al
Water St
Atlantic St
Church St
Meeting St
Tradd St
Ford Crt
Price's Al
Weims Crt
Ladson St
Lamboll St
King St
Legare St
Lenwood St
S Battery
E Battery
Murray Blvd

★ TOP EXPERIENCE

Old Slave Mart Museum

On the grounds of an open-air market that once auctioned African American men, women and children, this simple but powerful museum spotlights the realities and horrors of the trade in enslaved people in the years leading up to the Civil War. It was the largest of 40 or so similar auction houses in the city.

MAP P38 **D3**

PLANNING TIP
Combine a visit here with a trip to Johns Island to tour **McLeod Plantation**, where guides discuss plantation-era life from the perspective of both plantation owners and the enslaved.

Scan this QR code for further information.

Realities of the Slave Trade

With its grand homes and manicured gardens, Charleston is not short of aesthetic charms. But the city owes its beauty and success to an economy that was once driven by the labor of enslaved people. Charleston was the nation's slave trade capital, and millions of enslaved people entered the country via the port here. In fact, by 1860, 57% of the residents of South Carolina were enslaved.

This small **museum** *($7; 9am-5pm Mon-Sat)* is located inside a former auction complex known as Ryan's Mart that was in operation for seven years in the mid-1800s. Exhibits offer a no-holds-barred look at the business of the slave trade, and they take a deep dive into the day-to-day realities of traders, plantation owners and the enslaved. Within the museum's brick walls you'll also see exhibits that need little explanation, including whips, shackles and a deed of sale for auctioned human beings.

Firsthand Stories

Take a moment to listen to the recorded oral recollections of Elijah Green, who was born into slavery in Charleston in 1843. He shares stories

JOANNE DALE/SHUTTERSTOCK ©

about his family and also about the cruelties of one local slave owner. Green was interviewed in 1937 as part of a Works Progress Administration program during the Great Depression.

A Sense of Place

As you explore Charleston, keep in mind that the city prospered as a result of the work of the enslaved laborers who were forcibly brought here by ship. Their stories and those of their descendants are showcased at the new International African American Museum (p52) and, increasingly across the city.

QUICK BREAK
Walk over to **Harken Cafe & Bakery** *(harkencafe.com)* to discuss the exhibits over coffee or lunch.

WALKING TOUR

Walk South of Broad

Three hundred years of history jostle for attention between Broad St and the Battery, which means wandering off course is entirely expected. Sights include old-world gas lanterns, 18th-century cannons and scads of historic homes. A word of warning: if you stop to read every historic plaque you will take weeks to finish this walk.

START	END	LENGTH
Old Exchange & Provost Dungeon	Four Corners of Law/ St Michael's Church	1.5 miles; 1 hour

1 Revolutionary Dungeon

Begin at the **Old Exchange & Provost Dungeon**, where costumed guides lead tours of the dungeon where Stede Bonnet, the Gentleman Pirate, and Revolutionary War prisoners were once held.

2 Rainbow Row

Walk south to the pastel beauty of **Rainbow Row**, a block of redone 1730s merchant stores that inspired the birth of the Charleston Preservation Society, along with the preservation of the entire city in the 1920s.

3 Heyward-Washington House

Follow Tradd St to Church St and turn right. The **Heyward-Washington House**, where the first president slumbered in 1791, is on your left.

4 Edmondston-Alston House

Double back along Church St to take Water St and East Battery St to the **Edmondston-Alston House**, where docent-led tours take guests through public rooms to view intricate woodwork and family artifacts.

5 Battery & White Point Garden

Walk south to approach the **Battery & White Point Garden**, named for the fortifications that lined the seafront and for the mounds of oyster shells once piled over the point.

6 Williams Mansion

Cut through the park and make your way north along Meeting St to the **Williams Mansion**, formerly known as the Calhoun Mansion. This Gilded Age manor is Charleston's largest single-family residence and known for its opulent decor. Tours were paused during the pandemic but are scheduled to resume in spring 2025.

7 Nathaniel Russell House

Continuing north, the **Nathaniel Russell House** will appear on the left, and a tour here is worthwhile for its square-oval-rectangle footprint and free-flying spiral staircase. Don't miss the joggling board (p45) in the backyard.

8 St Michael's Church

At your final stop, notice **St Michael's Church** (71 Broad St) on the southeastern corner, representing God's law. With the city hall, the county courthouse and a federal courthouse sitting on the other corners, the intersection is known as the **Four Corners of Law**. St Michael's is the oldest church in town, and its bells have been announcing hurricanes, fires and attacks on the city for more than 250 years. Sweetgrass baskets are often for sale along Meeting St here.

EXPERIENCES

Learn about Washington's Travels at the Heyward-Washington House HISTORIC BUILDING

MAP: 1 P38 **D5**

Follow in the footsteps of George Washington within this **Georgian-style town house** *(charlestonmuseum.org; adult/child $15/12)*, which is named in part for America's first president. Washington rented the home for a week while touring the nation in 1791. Self-guided audio tours stop in what was likely his bedroom. The first owner, Thomas Heyward Jr, was one of four South Carolinians to sign the Declaration of Independence.

Furnishings include a chair that belonged to General Francis Marion (the 'Swamp Fox') and the priceless Holmes bookcase, which was declared on *Antiques Roadshow* to be the most magnificent piece of furniture in America. Exhibits also spotlight the lives of the enslaved workers who lived and worked on the property.

Bump Elbows with Locals over Wine & Cheese RESTAURANT

MAP: 2 P38 **B4**

Some think the staff can be a bit, well, brisk at **Gaulart & Maliclet** *(fastandfrenchcharleston.com; main dishes $23-28)*. But locals don't mind. They love to crowd around the shared tables at this tiny spot, also known as 'Fast & French,' to enjoy Gallic cheeses and sausages, fondues and an international array of entrées at night. It is particularly busy at lunch, famed for its daily special, which includes bread, soup, a main dish and wine for only $15.

Pause Beside Rainbow Row AREA

With its **13 candy-colored houses**, this stretch of Georgian row houses (MAP: 3 P38 **D5**) on lower E Bay St is catnip for social media feeds and one of the most photographed areas in Charleston. The structures date to 1730, when they served as merchant stores on the wharf, a sketchy part of town at the time. Starting in the 1920s the buildings were restored and painted over in pastels. People dug it, and soon much of the rest of Charleston was getting a similar makeover. Don't miss the **Tavern at Rainbow Row** *(facebook.com/thetaverncharleston)* (MAP: 4 P38 **E4**) just north on Bay St. The shop is America's oldest liquor store – it's been selling spirits since 1686! Check its Facebook page for details of free tastings of local bourbons, held every month or so.

Admire Architectural Prowess at the Nathaniel Russell House HISTORIC BUILDING

MAP: 5 P38 **C6**

This 1808 **Federal-style house** *(historiccharleston.org/house-museums/nathaniel-russell-house; adult/child $15/7)* holds a gorgeous surprise: a spectacular, self-supporting spiral staircase. And its beauty can only be fully appreciated by looking straight up. The home's namesake, and its first owner, was originally from Rhode Island, and he was known in Charleston as 'King of the Yankees.' Today, its meticulous restoration honors the finest details, such as the 1000 sheets of 22-karat gold leaf in the withdrawing room. Twenty layers of wall paint were peeled back to uncover the original colors, and handmade, fitted, contoured rugs were imported from the UK, as was originally done by the Russells. The small but lush **English garden** is also notable, as is the square-oval-rectangle footprint of the home.

Stroll the Battery & White Point Garden GARDENS

MAP: 6 P38 **C8**

The **Battery** is the southern tip of the Charleston Peninsula, buffered by a seawall. Walk the promenade along the seawall and scan the harbor for Fort Sumter. Live oaks provide shade for cannons and statues of military heroes in the adjacent garden. Flanked by historic homes and the harbor, the area is a pretty spot to relax.

JOGGLING BOARD

In the backyard of the Nathaniel Russell House you'll find a fine specimen of a super-Charlestonian porch furnishing – the joggling board. A 16ft plank set on rockers, it was apparently used in the early 1800s to cure rheumatoid arthritis and aid in courtship. Take a seat to understand.

Get Spooked at the Old Exchange & Provost Dungeon HISTORIC BUILDING

MAP: 7 P38 **E4**

The creepy **dungeon** inside this Colonial-era building *(oldexchange.org; adult/child $16/12)* is a stark reminder that South Carolinians had tough decisions to make in the years leading up to the Revolutionary War. The cramped space was used as a prison for American patriots held by the British during the conflict – and it doesn't look like a place where you'd want to spend an extended amount of time. That being said, kids will likely

COMBO TICKETS FOR TOURS

The Charleston Museum and the Historic Charleston Foundation sell ticket bundles that will save you a few dollars if you visit more than one historic home. The **Charleston Museum** *(charlestonmuseum.org)* offers tours of the Heyward-Washington House, the Joseph Manigault House and the Charleston Museum. **Historic Charleston Foundation** *(historiccharleston.org)* sells tickets to the Nathaniel Russell House and the Aiken-Rhett House. Note, however, that unless you're an antiques fanatic, much of the information is repeated.

BEST ROOFTOP BARS IN THE FRENCH QUARTER

Pavilion Bar
MAP: 10 P38 **D1**
With an infinity pool, illuminated umbrellas and stunning city views, this chic bar attracts a well-heeled set. The pool covered with plexiglass converts into a dance floor.

Rooftop at the Vendue
MAP: 11 P38 **E3**
This watering hole has sweet views of downtown, and happy-hour specials from 4pm to 6pm Sunday to Thursday.

Henry's on the Market
MAP: 12 P38 **D1**
It's not the swankiest of the lot, but this place earns kudos for proximity to Charleston City Market. It sits atop Henry's, the oldest continuous restaurant in the state, dating to 1932.

enjoy it. The dungeon sits beneath a stately **Georgian Palladian customs house** completed in 1771. Costumed guides lead the 25-minute dungeon tour, and exhibits about the history of the city are displayed on the upper floors.

Listen to the Bells at St Michael's Church

CHURCH

MAP: 8 P38 **C4**

St Michael's is the oldest church in town, dating back to 1752, and its beloved bells have been announcing the time and various events, including earthquakes, hurricanes, fires and attacks on the city, for more than 250 years. John Rutledge and Charles Cotesworth Pinckney (both of whom signed the US Constitution) are buried here.

Shop Local Merchants at Charleston City Market

MARKET

MAP: 9 P38 **C1**

More than 300 vendors hawk everything from sweetgrass baskets to piping-hot biscuits inside this vibrant, **open-air market** (*thecharlestoncitymarket.com; 9:30am-5pm*). Started in 1804, locals say they wouldn't be caught dead in this tourist-filled spot, and some travelers may feel it's a bit schlocky. Locally made products (marked with a 'Certified Authentic Handmade in Charleston' seal) include Charleston Tea Garden teas and Old Whaling Co soaps.

The **night market** (*6:30-9:30pm Fri & Sat*) is held in the same space and displays the wares of more than 100 local artists and craftspeople.

WALKING TOURS

Charleston Footprints (*charlestonfootprints.com; $28.50*) offers an excellent walking tour of historical sights led by a knowledgeable and theatrical local. **Bulldog Tours** (*bulldogtours.com; adult/child $37/27*) also has fantastic guides for these neighborhoods.

LISTINGS

Best Places for...

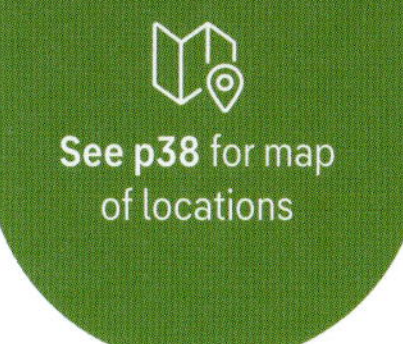

$ Budget $$ Midrange $$$ Top End

Eating

Seafood

Fleet Landing $$

13 F2

The perfect Charleston lunch: a river view, a cup of she-crab soup with a splash of sherry, and a bowl of shrimp and grits. *11am-3:30pm & 5-10pm, bar open all day*

Sandwiches

Brown Dog Deli $

D4

Gourmet sandwiches packed with creative ingredients. The Folly Beach Crunch is stuffed with turkey, bacon and cheddar, sea salt chips and guacamole. *9am-6pm Mon-Sat, to 4pm Sun*

Southern Fare

Slightly North of Broad $$$

E2

Tried-and-true French Quarter mainstay with a rotating menu of Low-country comfort dishes reinvented with flair. *11am-2:30pm, from 5pm Mon-Fri, slightly longer hours Sat & Sun*

Brunch

High Cotton $$$

16 E2

A jazz band keeps the scene lively at this spot on weekends. Scallops with stone-ground grits are recommended. *5:30-10pm Mon-Thu, to 11pm Fri, 10am-11pm Sat, 10am-10pm Sun*

Drinking

Pub

Blind Tiger

D4

In a building that dates to 1893, this atmospheric bar seduces with good pub grub. Enjoy your cocktail in the expansive back courtyard. *4-11pm Mon-Thu, 11am-midnight Fri & Sat, 11am-11pm Sun*

Cocktails

Palmetto Lobby Bar

E2

Cocktails topped with alcohol-infused foam are a kick at this stylish hotel bar. *4-11pm Mon-Thu, 11am-midnight Fri & Sat, 11am-11pm Sun*

Coffee

Harken Cafe & Bakery

19 C3

Cozy spot for caffeinated drinks and an inviting line-up of pastries, bowls and salads. *7am-3pm Mon-Fri, 8am-3pm Sat, 8am-1pm Sun*

Shopping

Gallery

Robert Lange Studios

20 D3

Some of the city's best contemporary art regularly appears in this long-standing gallery. Artist Nathan Durfee's experimental work is a highlight. *11am-5pm*

Charleston Crafts Cooperative Gallery

21 E3

A well-edited selection of contemporary South Carolina–made crafts, such as sweetgrass baskets, hand-dyed silks and wood carvings. *10am-6pm*

See p68
for eating
and drinking
listings

Explore
East Side, NoMo & Hampton Park

Away from the heaviest tourist hubbub, the northern and eastern stretches of Charleston are fairly quiet, with several noteworthy attractions. The East Side is home to the new International African American Museum (IAAM), the Aiken-Rhett House and the Charleston Museum, as well as numerous top restaurants. It's also a jumping-off point for Fort Sumter. South Carolina Aquarium is great for kids and rainy days. Once an industrial area, NoMo (North Morrison) has more recently attracted tech companies and appealing restaurants, transforming it into a creative corridor. Residential Hampton Park holds the Citadel, plus expansive green spaces and some hyper-local cafes and breweries.

Getting Around

Walking

Sidewalks connect key sights in the East Side, and it's easy to stroll around the Citadel and Hampton Park.

Bus

CARTA bus 20 runs along Meeting St and bus 211 travels along King and Meeting Sts. The free College of Charleston/Aquarium DASH shuttle links the College of Charleston with the Liberty Sq area.

Bicycle

Lime now runs Charleston's bike-share program. There are e-bike stations near the visitor center and the International African American Museum.

Hampton Park (p65)

THE BEST

MUSEUM International African American Museum (p52)

GUIDED TOUR Aiken-Rhett House (p56)

HISTORY Fort Sumter & Fort Moultrie National Historic Park (p58)

BREWPUB Edmund's Oast (p64)

MEAL FIG (p68)

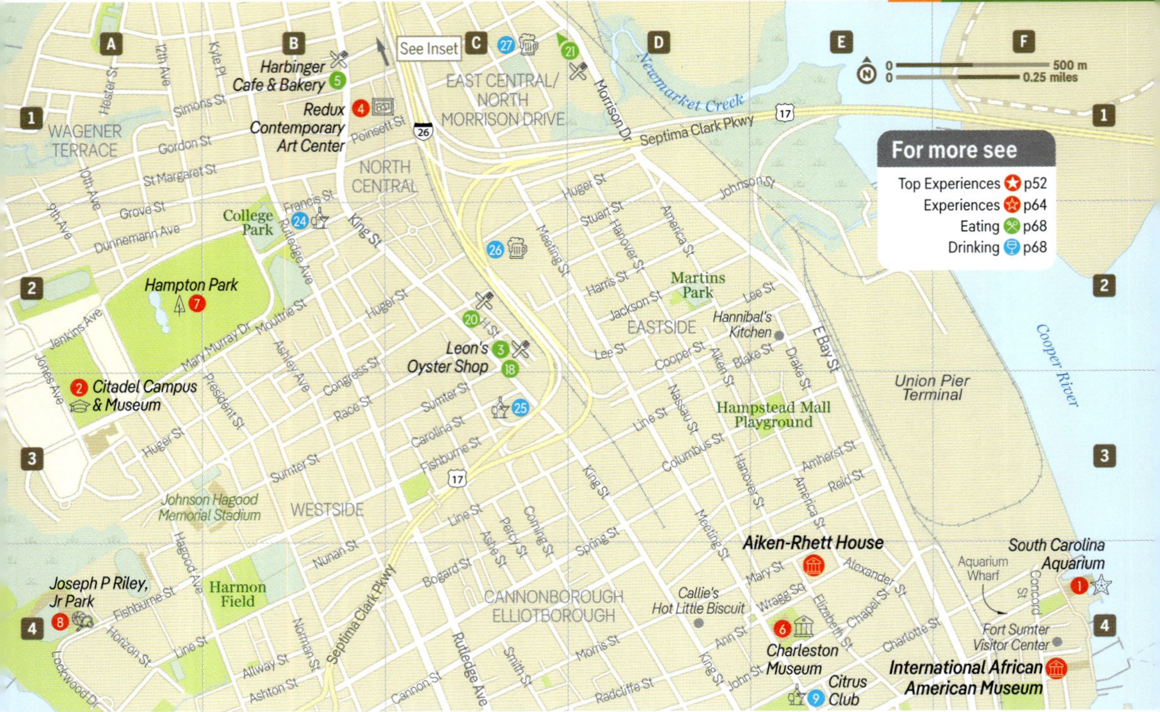

For more see
Top Experiences p52
Experiences p64
Eating p68
Drinking p68

0 500 m
0 0.25 miles

See Inset

1 Harbinger Cafe & Bakery 5
Redux Contemporary Art Center 4
Hampton Park 7
Citadel Campus & Museum 2
College Park 24
Leon's Oyster Shop 3 18
20
21
25
26
27
Joseph P Riley, Jr Park 8
Harmon Field
Johnson Hagood Memorial Stadium
Martins Park
Hannibal's Kitchen
Hampstead Mall Playground
Union Pier Terminal
Aiken-Rhett House
Callie's Hot Little Biscuit
Charleston Museum 6
Citrus Club 9
South Carolina Aquarium 1
Aquarium Wharf
Fort Sumter Visitor Center
International African American Museum

WAGENER TERRACE
NORTH CENTRAL
EAST CENTRAL/ NORTH MORRISON DRIVE
EASTSIDE
WESTSIDE
CANNONBOROUGH ELLIOTBOROUGH

Newmarket Creek
Cooper River

Hester St
12th Ave
Kyle Pl
Simons St
Gordon St
St Margaret St
10th Ave
9th Ave
Grove St
Dunnemann Ave
Jenkins Ave
Jones Ave
Mary Murray Dr
Moultrie St
Rutledge Ave
Francis St
Poinsett St
King St
Huger St
Ashley Ave
Congress St
Race St
President St
Sumter St
Carolina St
Fishburne St
H St
Meeting St
Stuart St
Hanover St
America St
Harris St
Jackson St
Lee St
Cooper St
Aiken St
Blake St
Drake St
E Bay St
Johnson St
Morrison Dr
Septima Clark Pkwy
Line St
Nassau St
Columbus St
Amherst St
Reid St
Spring St
Coming St
Percy St
Ashe St
Bogard St
Nunan St
Hagood Ave
Norman St
Allway St
Ashton St
Cannon St
Smith St
Morris St
Radcliffe St
John St
Ann St
Mary St
Wragg Sq
Elizabeth St
Chapel St
Alexander St
Charlotte St
Concord St
Horizon St
Lockwood Dr
A B C D E F
1 2 3 4

North Charleseton
Magnolia Plantation
Drayton Hall
Charleston International Airport
Mark Clark Expwy
E Montague Ave
W Montague Ave
Bexley St
Jackrabbit Filly
Firefly Distillery
Savannah River
HL Hunley
Rivers Ave
Meeting St
Spruill Ave
Carner Ave
Dorchester Rd
Leeds Ave
Ashley River Rd
Bees Ferry Rd
Ashley River
Marty Utsey Park
Orange Grove Rd
Refinery
0 4 km
0 2 miles
Marion Square
Fiat Lux
RADCLIFFBOROUGH
HISTORIC DISTRICT
College of Charleston
University Hospital
Spring St
Cannon St
Bee St
Courtenay Dr
President St
Jonathan Lucas St
Ashley Ave
Mill St
Warren St
Vanderhorst St
Ogier St
Calhoun St
Smith St
Pitt St
Coming St
George St
St Philip St
King St
Burns La
Society St
Wentworth St
Hasell St
Anson St
E Bay St
Washington St
Laurens St
Concord St
N Market St
S Market St
Market St
Cumberland St
Vendue Range
Magazine St
Queen St
Chalmers St
State St
Broad St
Elliott St
Logan St
Legare St
Tradd St
Church St
Lenwood St
Water St
Atlantic St
Lamboll St
S Battery
E Battery
Murray Blvd
A B C D E F
5 6 7 8

★ TOP EXPERIENCE

International African American Museum

More than 250,000 enslaved Africans entered the United States in Charleston, and many disembarked at Gadsden's Wharf, now home to the striking new International African American Museum. The museum shares the stories of the African American diaspora through interactive exhibits, firsthand recollections and eye-catching artifacts.

MAP P50 **F4**

PLANNING TIP
Admission is by timed entry. Purchasing a ticket online before your visit is recommended. Tickets include access to the Center for Family History, a hub for genealogy research.

Scan this QR code to buy tickets.

Permanent Galleries

The **museum** *(iaamuseum.org; adult/child $22/10; 9am-5pm Tue-Sun, last entry 4pm)* tells the story of the African American diaspora, using touch-stones from South Carolina's history to illuminate the broader Black experience in America. These experiences are explored across 12 galleries and exhibition spaces. Your bags will be searched prior to entry. Set aside 90 minutes for your visit.

Begin your visit in the **American Journeys Gallery**, where life-size videos of Black historians and various professionals complement artifacts and exhibit panels about key moments in African American history. Topics include the US Supreme Court's 1896 *Plessy v Ferguson* decision enshrining the 'separate but equal' doctrine, the Great Migration, military service, the Civil Rights and Black Power movements and the election of Barack Obama.

From here, eight floor-to-ceiling video screens comprise the **Transatlantic Gallery**, an immersive introduction to the African diaspora that will funnel you to the remaining galleries.

Delve into the accomplishments of Black South Carolinians in the interactive **South Carolina Connections** gallery just ahead. A digital touch

ELLIS CREEK PHOTOGRAPHY ©

table anchors the space and lets visitors choose the stories they want to follow. A few steps away, **Gullah-Geechee culture** takes the spotlight – be sure to step into the re-created one-room Praise House and watch the short film about the uplifting Moving Hall Star Singers, a multigenerational gospel group from Johns Island. A Praise House was not a church but a musical gathering place where the community shared joyous songs of hope. A wooden bateau beside the Praise House showcases the importance of fishing to the Gullah-Geechee.

Exhibits in **African Roots & Routes** are calling cards for the many countries with ties to the African diaspora, which originated in West and East Central Africa. Two dark walls flank the gallery, one displaying the birth names and ages of Africans seized for enslavement and the other sharing the Anglicized names given after their

PARKING
Your best bet for parking is the city garage *(24 Calhoun St; per 30min $1)*. Called the **Aquarium Garage**, it's just a couple of blocks from the museum.

arrival in the United States. The **Carolina Gold/ Memories of the Enslaved Gallery** traces the economic impact of the labor of enslaved people – many from rice-growing West Africa – on South Carolina's many rice plantations.

Creative Journeys

Throughout the exhibit areas a variety of creative works, from poetry by Langston Hughes and Nikki Giovanni to paintings, musical performances and striking crafts, including a Gee's Bend quilt, add context and beauty as you explore. Much of the art is contemporary, providing a fresh look at important themes. A short, brilliantly styled film on a 30ft-high video screen in the **Atlantic Worlds** gallery video reveals the connections between Charleston, Barbados and Sierra Leone. An intricate Mardi Gras Indian suit, just a few steps away, is a colorful celebration of Fat Tuesday.

SEAN RAYFORD/STRINGER VIA GETTY IMAGES ©

Gardens & Building

Canary Island palms and green sweetgrass catch the eye in the **African American Memorial Garden**, which surrounds the museum building. Look carefully at the **Tide Tribute**, a ground-level memorial where relief figures emerge from pools of water as the tide recedes. These figures resemble the bodies of Africans brought to America by ship. The striking **museum building** is supported by 18 columns, which keep it 13ft above the hallowed ground of the wharf. The garden and memorial are free and open to the public.

Center for Family History

Visitors can trace their genealogy at the **Center for Family History**, where staff members are on hand to explain the center's research tools, all available on iPads. The center also offers monthly webinars and in-house programs to provide research strategies. An exhibit here shares details about Michelle Obama's Lowcountry ancestors.

Museum History

The museum was 20 years in the making, and its development met with some controversies along the way. Some questioned the location in a rapidly gentrifying area of the city instead of a regional Black community. Others responded that the ties to Ghadsens Wharf and Wraggsborough, which was where the Black community once thrived, were reason enough to choose this location.

There were also questions about the selection of Pei Cobb & Freed, an international architectural firm, as the lead design team instead of an African American architectural firm. Black architects were part of the final design team. And some puzzled over the stark design of the museum, which they argued feels more Northern European and isn't very Afrocentric.

QUICK BREAK
Hannibal's Kitchen
(hannibalkitchen.com; 11am-8pm Mon-Sat), 1 mile north, serves Gullah-Geechee standards like shrimp-and-crab rice (its signature dish). Opened by Robert 'Hannibal' Huger in 1985, the restaurant is now managed by his granddaughters.

★ TOP EXPERIENCE

Aiken-Rhett House

The only surviving urban town house complex, this 1820 abode gives a fascinating glimpse of antebellum life on a 45-minute audio tour. The role of the enslaved is emphasized and visitors wander into their dorm-style quarters before moving on to the lifestyle of Charleston's elite. The Historic Charleston Foundation has conserved but not restored the home, so you get peeling Parisian wallpaper and all.

MAP P50 **E4**

PLANNING TIP
A combo ticket for the Aiken-Rhett and Nathaniel Russell Houses *($24, valid six months)* will save you $6. The museum is open from 10am to 5pm; last admission is at 4:15pm.

Scan this QR code for information and tickets.

Main House

Stepping through the ornate doors of this tangerine-colored **mansion** *(historiccharleston.org/house-museums/aiken-rhett-house; adult/child $15/7)* feels a bit like time-traveling to 1858. Not much has changed inside former South Carolina Governor William Aiken's home, and the collection of books, furnishings, art and architectural details, though worn, is largely intact. Some will find it a bit too *Great Expectations*; others will simply enjoy gawking at the peeling wallpaper, cracked plaster and chamber pots.

Regardless, a stroll through the home offers insight into evolving architectural tastes in the first half of the 19th century. The upper floors exemplify the late Federal period with their careful woodwork and symmetrical proportions, while the main floor and marble staircase have been renovated in the Greek Revival style. The art gallery, added in 1858, recalls the Victorian era.

Slave Quarters

The Aiken-Rhett House is often referred to as an urban plantation, and it's no secret that enslaved people lived and toiled here as cooks, laundresses, footmen, seamstresses, gardeners and the like. Four-teen enslaved people are thought to have occupied

STEPHEN TAYLOR/ALAMY STOCK PHOTO ©

the cramped 2nd-story quarters at the back of the home and to have shared a communal kitchen. Careful analysis has suggested that the rooms had fireplaces and were painted in bright colors.

More recently, an archaeological dig in the property's laundry room yielded some promising finds, including egg shells, fish scales, bottles and ceramics. The items offer insight into the daily lives of the enslaved, and some are on display on a viewing platform in the laundry room.

Annual Flair

During recent **Charleston Festivals** local interior designers have been invited to re-imagine some of the rooms in the home. The rules? Furniture cannot be moved and art cannot be placed on walls. The resulting 'Designer Vignettes' have reflected the visions of quite varied imaginations, with displays ranging from the whimsical to the floral.

QUICK BREAK
King St is just a couple of blocks away, with plenty of options for dining and drinking. Pop into **Callie's Hot Little Biscuit** for the quintessential Charleston snack.

★ TOP EXPERIENCE

Fort Sumter & Fort Moultrie National Historic Park

Grab a seat on the upper deck for the breezy ferry ride across Charleston Harbor to Fort Sumter, where the first shots of the Civil War were fired. Across the harbor on Sullivan's Island, Fort Moultrie is also part of this new national historic park. Together the fortifications illuminate the power struggles that plagued the harbor through four major wars.

MAP P50 **F4**

GETTING THERE
The only way to get to Fort Sumter is by a 30-minute boat tour *(adult/child $37/23)* from Liberty Sq or Patriot's Point. You can drive to Fort Moultrie on Sullivan's Island.

Fort Sumter

As you'll see from the ferry, the fort itself isn't physically imposing or visually impressive, but if you have even a passing interest in American history, a trip to Sumter is requisite. The fort is named after Revolutionary War patriot Thomas Sumter, and its construction on an artificial island, in large part undertaken by enslaved laborers and craftspeople, began in 1829. Its 5ft-thick brick walls towered about 50ft over the water and supported several tiers of weaponry, though they were still unfinished in 1860 when federal troops moved in.

Fort Sumter Under Attack

On April 12, 1861, Confederate forces fired on the fort, and less than two days later the Union surrendered. The port of Charleston became a loophole in the blockade of the Atlantic coast, allowing the Confederacy to receive needed supplies and to continue exporting cotton. They held it for nearly four years, until General William T Sherman and his troops forced an evacuation in 1865. The fort was mostly unused until it became a national monument in 1948.

AK1013/SHUTTERSTOCK ©

Your Visit

Upon arrival you'll disembark the ferry and walk to the fort. Travelers on the first ferry of the day may be asked to help raise the US flag, while those on the last may be asked to lower it. National park rangers and docents are available on-site to answer questions and share information about the history of the fort and its role in the Civil War. You'll have about an hour to wander the site and its small museum. A map provided by the park can help you decide how to spend your time.

Fort Sumter Visitor Education Center

Most boat tours to Fort Sumter leave from Liberty Sq, home of the Fort Sumter Visitor Education Center. (The other jumping-off point is Patriot's Point in Mount Pleasant.) The visitor center offers free exhibits about the roots of conflict that

PARK REDESIGNATION

Formerly two separate national-park entities, Fort Sumter and Fort Moultrie were redesignated a single national historic park in 2019. The new park also includes the Sullivan's Island Life Saving Station Historic District.

led to South Carolina's secession, the Civil War and the war's aftermath. Open daily from 8:30am to 5pm, it's a good primer before you jump on the boat. It also provides a concise introduction to the story of the fort for those who don't have time for the tour.

Fort Moultrie

Although it's not as famous as Fort Sumter, Fort Moultrie actually offers a deeper dive into the region's coastal defense systems, as its exhibits and structures span nearly 200 years. The fort standing today is the third version of Moultrie, and a very different structure than the first, which was composed of palmetto logs that held back the British in 1776. The site of that old fort is to the west of the present-day fort.

EWY MEDIA/SHUTTERSTOCK ©

Outside the Walls

Other attractions outside the walls include the site of the second Fort Moultrie, which was destroyed by a hurricane in 1801. There's also a cannon walk, which showcases artillery pieces from the Civil War, and a burial site for Seminole leader Osceola, who died at the fort in 1838. Kids and dogs will love to play on the fine white sands and climb the rocks on the adjacent beach.

Inside the Fort

Visitors can check out a WWII harbor command post, a couple of batteries designed in the early 1900s to protect the mine field, an exhibit on the modernization of weapons in 1870 and a display about the sweeping technological changes that happened during the Civil War. There's enough here to keep you busy for several hours, particularly if you're a history buff.

Fort Moultrie Visitor Center

If you have questions, walk across the street from the fort to the visitor center, which has an information desk staffed by park rangers, along with a theater, a museum and a bookstore. Definitely check out the 22-minute documentary about Fort Moultrie and the coastal defense system. It begins every half-hour in the theater.

You can conquer the museum here in about 30 minutes. It includes artifacts and exhibits about the American Revolution, the Civil War, WWI and WWII. (The fort evolved to meet the needs of each of these conflicts.) There's also some information about the Sullivan's Island trade in enslaved people. Walk up to the rooftop deck for views across Charleston Harbor.

AN OFFICER & A GENTLEMAN

Pierre Beauregard, the Confederate general who commanded the attack on Fort Sumter, had been a student of Major Robert Anderson, the Union commander defending the fort, at West Point. Communications between the two men before the siege demonstrate the utmost respect.

Walk the East Side

A walk through the busy East Side reveals Charleston's complicated history while offering a glimpse of the city's future. Historic homes and churches are plentiful, but trendy new hotels and their sleek rooftop bars are currently catnip for social media feeds. This walk ends beside the Cooper River at a compelling new museum earning international acclaim.

START	END	LENGTH
Charleston Visitor Center	International African American Museum	1.7 miles; 1½ hours

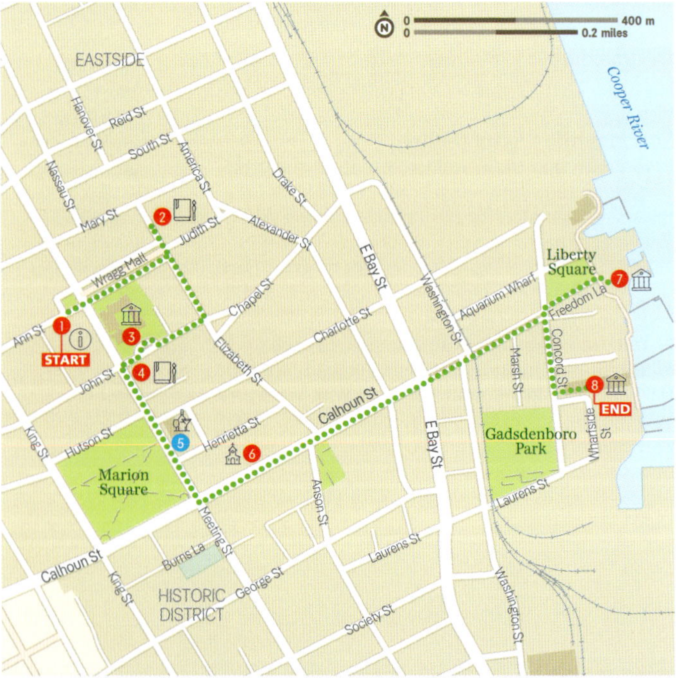

1 Information Hub

Pick up maps and brochures at the **Charleston Visitor Center**, which occupies a former railroad building constructed in the mid-1800s. There's a large parking lot here too.

2 House of 1820s Splendor

Follow Ann St one block east to the **Aiken-Rhett House** (p56). With its tangerine-bright exterior and large porches, this 19th-century town house is hard to miss. Tours explore the home, preserved 'as found.' Walk south and turn right onto John St.

3 Unexpected Exhibits

For a quick introduction to the city's history, pop into the **Charleston Museum** (p65). A few quirky exhibits – a stuffed polar bear and a whale skeleton – add some fun. Walk south on Meeting St.

4 Historic Home

Once the showpiece of a French Huguenot rice planter, the three-story, Federal-style **Joseph Manigault House** dates from 1803. There's a tiny neoclassical gate temple in the garden, and the house is full of 19th-century furnishings.

5 Citrus Club

Step into the elevator at the trendy Dewberry Hotel for a ride up to the **Citrus Club** *(thedewberry charleston.com)*. Greenery is abundant and gathering areas are cozy at this rooftop bar, and the bird's-eye view of the city is superb.

6 Worship & Remembrance

Walk east on Calhoun St to **Mother Emanuel African Methodist Episcopal Church**. Established in 1816, it is Charleston's oldest Black church and its steeple is a city landmark. The church was the site of a 2015 mass shooting in which the pastor and eight churchgoers were murdered.

7 Road to War

Brush up on Civil War history at the free **Fort Sumter Visitor Center at Liberty Square** *(8:30am-4:30pm)*. This small national-park museum overlooks the Cooper River and doubles as the take-off point for **ferries** *(adult/child $37/23)* to the fort.

8 Black History

Walk south to explore the gardens and Tide Tribute memorial outside the new **International African American Museum** (p52), which rises above historic Gadsden's Wharf. Here, thousands of enslaved people disembarked after surviving the Middle Passage voyage from Africa. The gardens and memorials are free to enter.

EXPERIENCES

Spend a Rainy Day at the Aquarium

AQUARIUM

MAP: 1 P50 **F4**

The waterfront **South Carolina Aquarium** *(scaquarium.org; adult/child $36/29)* is an ode to South Carolina's wildlife, with creatures hailing from the mountain forest, piedmont, salt marsh, coastal and undersea habitats. Although the facility is smaller than some of the country's more prominent aquariums, there are plenty of fish and other creatures. Noteworthy residents include a bald eagle, a gopher tortoise, river otters and sharks. The sea-turtle rehabilitation wing is a huge hit with both kids and adults. Holiday lights illuminate various installations during the **Aquarium Aglow** festivities in November and December.

Watch a Citadel Parade

SCHOOL

MAP: 2 P50 **A3**

It can be a bit unnerving how polite and helpful everyone is on the campus of **The Citadel** *(citadel.edu)*, a military college set in historic Romanesque buildings and replete with military memorials. But good manners are rather refreshing in today's busy world.

One campus highlight is the **Friday afternoon dress parade**, when the uniformed corps of cadets gathers on 10-acre Summerall Field to march, conduct drills and hold ceremonies. Parades begin at 3:45pm most Fridays and are open to the public.

There's a small **museum** on the 3rd floor of the campus library that displays mostly military apparel and a re-creation of historic barracks. You'll find an interactive campus map, with details about various buildings and memorials, on the school website.

Enjoy Good Times at Leon's

RESTAURANT

MAP: 3 P50 **C2**

So this is where everybody is. In an old body shop reimagined as an industrial-chic eatery, **Leon's Oyster Shop** *(leonsoystershop.com)* is a Charleston favorite for three distinct and delicious items: oysters, fried chicken and scalloped potatoes. There's no better place to eat off a hangover, and the rosé on tap is a classy way to keep the party going.

Admire Creativity at Redux

ARTS CENTER

For up-to-the-minute art, take a moment to wander the every-changing exhibits at this **contemporary-art center** and event space (MAP: 4 P50 **B1**; *reduxstudios.org*) near Hampton Park, home to three galleries and a few dozen studios. Fuel up afterward with a coffee and pastry from nearby **Harbinger Cafe & Bakery** (MAP: 5 P50 **B1**).

Delve into the Charleston Museum MUSEUM

MAP: 6 P50 **E4**

The **Charleston Museum** *(charlestonmuseum.org; adult/youth/child $15/12/6)* may be the oldest museum in the country – it opened in 1773 – but it certainly isn't stuffy. Old chamber pots in the women's bathroom are a fun distraction, and the famous stuffed polar bear is a nod to the museum's earliest days, when any curiosity was fair game for an exhibit.

An hour-long visit is a good introduction to the city if you're looking for background before strolling through the Historic District. Exhibits spotlight various periods of Charleston's long and storied past. Artifacts include a whale skeleton, slave tags and the 'secession table' used for the signing of the state's secession documents before the Civil War. *Beyond the Ashes: The Lowcountry's New Beginnings* is a new permanent exhibit. The museum is open daily from 9am to 5pm.

Chill out at Hampton Park PARK

MAP: 7 P50 **A2**

This big, awesome **park** is beloved for its arboreal and floral displays, fitness trail and large swaths of open space, often used for things like Frisbee matches. It has public restrooms and parking, and is rarely crowded.

BARBECUE SMACKDOWN

Maybe it's because barbecue needs a lot of room to be prepared and enjoyed, but the city's best smoked-meat joints occupy expansive spaces in the northern part of town. In fact, three top spots are within a half-mile or so of each other. The heavy hitters? **Lewis Barbecue**, famed for its Texas-style brisket, and **Rodney Scott's BBQ**, known for its pulled pork. Both earn well-deserved national kudos – and long lines. But take note: locals will tell you that they enjoy **Home Team BBQ**, which draws convivial crowds on the regular, as much as they like the big boys.

Root for the RiverDogs BASEBALL

MAP: 8 P50 **A4**

Watch fireworks explode over the diamond on Friday nights at **Joseph P Riley, Jr Park**, the home of the **RiverDogs** *(milb.com/charleston)* minor-league baseball team and the Citadel team. The stadium is named for a longtime former Charleston mayor who regularly attends games, but it's more often referred to as 'the Joe'. Bill Murray is part-owner and Director of Fun of the RiverDogs.

BEST OF NORTH CHARLESTON
The fast-growing city of North Charleston is a 5-mile drive from downtown, and it's home to an increasingly interesting collection of restaurants, watering holes and other must-tries.

Jackrabbit Filly

MAP: 11 P50 **D6**
The Sichuan hot *karaage* – a fiery fried-chicken dish – is fantastic at this hip Chinese-American restaurant also known for its cocktails.

Firefly Distillery

MAP: 12 P50 **D6**
Recently relocated from Wadmalaw Island, Firefly serves the world's first handcrafted sweet-tea-flavored vodka. Popular live music venue too.

HL Hunley

MAP: 13 P50 **D7**
Displays the wreckage of the world's first successful combat submarine, which sank off the coast in 1864. Open weekends.

Relax on a Rooftop Patio

SCENIC BARS

The cool thing about Charleston's rooftop bars? There may be lines to get in on occasion, but for the most part, too-cool attitudes are low. This isn't LA or NYC, y'all. A bright neon orange overlooks the bar at the ever-stylish **Citrus Club** (MAP: 9 P50 **E4**; *thedewberrycharleston.com*), which has sweeping views of the Holy City's church steeples, Marion Park and the Ravenel Bridge from its perch atop the Dewberry hotel. There are plenty of sofas and comfy chairs for lounging. Around the corner, admire the artwork beside the lobby before gliding up to the **Fiat Lux** (MAP: 10 P50 **E5**; *hotelbennett.com/dining-and-lounges/fiat-lux*) at the Hotel Bennett, where you'll enjoy views of Marion Park with your cocktails.

Catch a Show at the Refinery

LIVE MUSIC

MAP: 14 P50 **D8**
A cool breeze, great bands and a welcoming attitude. Yep, **The Refinery** (*therefinerychs.com*) is a special place to watch live music. Check the calendar for upcoming shows at this 2000-person outdoor venue beside the railroad tracks just north of North Morrison and North Charleston. Recent acts include Molly Tuttle, Infamous Stringdusters, Greensky Bluegrass and the Black Pumas. Other tenants in this creativity hub include **The Whale**, a bar with a lengthy craft-beer list, and the sports bar **Cleats**.

Magnolia Plantation

Visit Ashley River Plantations HISTORIC BUILDINGS

Three significant plantations line the Ashley River about a 20-minute drive from downtown Charleston. All offer talks and tours concerning the role of slavery.

Of the three on the Ashley River, **Drayton Hall** (MAP: 15 P50 **A6**; *draytonhall.org; adult/youth/child $32/18/14*) is the best for history buffs, as it features the oldest plantation house open to the public in America. **Magnolia Plantation** (MAP: 16 P50 **A6**; *magnoliaplantation.com; adult/youth/child $32/18/14)* has great tours, wild gardens and a swamp trail, all with a Disney vibe. **Middleton Place** (MAP: 17 P50 **A6**; *middletonplace.org; adult/youth/child $32/15/10*) has the country's oldest, most elegant gardens and a fancy restaurant and hotel. You'll be hard-pressed to find the time to visit all three in one day, but you could squeeze in two (allow a couple of hours for each).

Ashley River Rd is also known as SC 61, which can be reached from downtown Charleston via Hwy 17. Check the venues' websites before visiting to confirm they're not closed for an event.

LISTINGS

Best Places for...

$ Budget $$ Midrange $$$ Top End

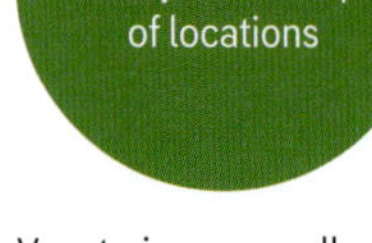

Eating

Bakeries

Welton's Tiny Bakeshop $

18 C2

Lines stretch out the door – but move fast – at this aptly named bakery, where four customers max can squeeze inside. Admire the kolaches, croissants and cookies once you're in. *8am-1pm Wed-Sat*

Sushi

167 Sushi Bar $$

19 F5

Enjoy sushi rolls, dumplings and rice and noodle dishes at this tiny hole-in-the-wall, the former home of sister restaurant **167 Raw**. *noon-10pm Mon-Wed, to 10:30pm Thu-Sat*

Pub Food

Little Jack's Tavern $

20 C2

A classy neighborhood cocktail bar and restaurant, with one helluva hamburger. *noon-10pm*

Edmund's Oast $$

21 D1

Occupying a former hardware store in NoMo, Charleston's highest-brow brewpub serves Southern faves and a long list of cocktails and draft beers. *11am-10pm*

Southern

FIG $$$

22 E6

A foodie favorite since 2003 that's known for welcoming staff, efficient but unrushed service and sustainably sourced nouvelle Southern fare from James Beard Award winner Mike Lata. *5-10:30pm Tue-Sat*

New American

Zero Café + Bar $$$

23 F5

Food Network chef Vinson Petrillo assumes his diners are intrepid and sends out dainty plates of pressure-cooked octopus, ricotta *gnudi* (gnocchi-like dumplings) and scallop tartare. Vegetarians are well looked after. *6-10pm Tue-Sun*

Drinking

Sports Bar

Moe's Crosstown Tavern

24 B2

Considered Hampton Park's best dive bar, this place fills with loyal patrons on game days. Enjoy burgers, Sunday brunch and camaraderie. *11am-2am*

Dive Bar

Recovery Room

25 C3

Late-night dive that often swells with college students and boozy regulars in search of cheap whiskey. Has various theme nights and sells more Pabst Blue Ribbon beer (commonly abbreviated PBR) than any other bar in the US. *2pm-2am Mon-Fri, noon-2am Sat & Sun*

167 Raw

BOB PARDUE - SC/ALAMY STOCK PHOTO ©

Breweries

Palmetto Brewing Company

 C2

Charleston's first microbrewery (since Prohibition, anyway) produces four main craft beers with fresh barley malts and hops: an amber ale, a pilsner and a couple of IPAs. *4-10pm Mon-Thu, noon-10pm Sat, noon 7pm Sun*

Revelry Brewery Co

 C1

Knock back artfully crafted cold ones on the fairy-lit and fire-pit-heated rooftop, which affords expansive views all the way to the Ravenel Bridge. *noon-10pm Mon-Thu, noon-11pm Fri & Sat, noon-8pm Sun*

Edmund's Oast Brewing Co

 D8

Just north of Edmund's Oast Restaurant in NoMo, this no-pretense brewery is set in a 20,000-sq-ft facility with 26 boozy beverages on tap. *11am-9pm*

See p80
for eating
and drinking
listings

Explore Harleston Village, King Street & Cannonborough Elliottborough

College students, young professionals and families infuse these three neighborhoods with palpable energy. Harleston Village feels the most suburban of the three, but it's also home to the College of Charleston campus. King St, with Upper and Lower sections, is densely packed with hit-or-miss restaurants, upscale boutiques, cute bookstores and loft-style condos. The Cannonborough Elliottborough area attracts young creatives and families with its fixed-up Victorians and independent businesses. Places of worship, galleries and coffee shops are prevalent, and there are a number of eclectic restaurants and cafes.

Getting Around

Walking

Sidewalks are prevalent, but traffic can be heavy, with numerous out-of-town drivers. Obey pedestrian traffic signals.

Bus

Bus 210, the College of Charleston/Aquarium DASH, connects the College of Charleston with the Aquarium. Bus 211, the Meeting/King DASH, travels King St. Both are free.

Car

Driving is convenient, but on-street parking can be hard to find. Never park in the St Philip Street Garage by the College of Charleston during busy school hours.

THE BEST

FOR CONTEMPLATION Gateway Walk (p76)

LOCAL GIFTS Preservation Society of Charleston (p76)

SEAFOOD Ordinary (p76)

BEER SAMPLING Charleston Brews Cruise (p78)

ART BREAK Gibbes Museum (p76)

King Street (p74)
JEFFREY GREENBERG/UNIVERSAL IMAGES GROUP VIA GETTY IMAGES ©

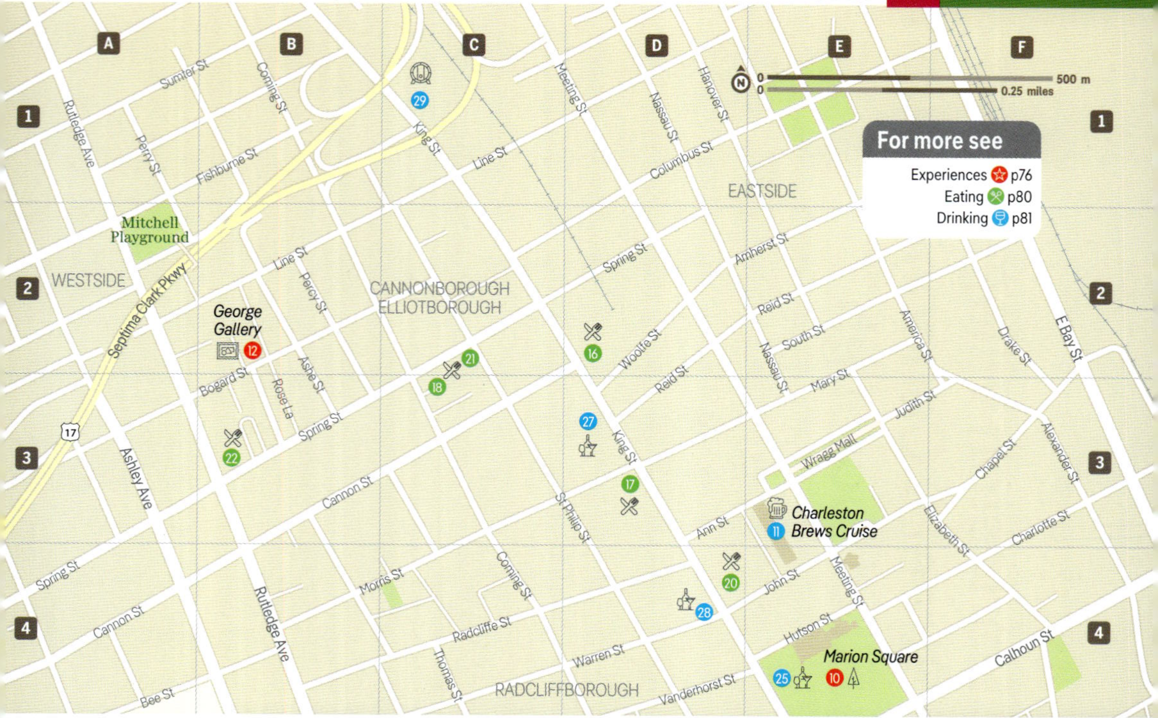

For more see
Experiences p76
Eating p80
Drinking p81

Mitchell Playground
WESTSIDE
George Gallery 12
CANNONBOROUGH ELLIOTBOROUGH
EASTSIDE
Charleston Brews Cruise 11
Marion Square 10
RADCLIFFBOROUGH
16
17
18
20
21
22
25
27
28
29

Sumter St
Coming St
Rutledge Ave
Perry St
Fishburne St
King St
Line St
Meeting St
Nassau St
Hanover St
Columbus St
Septima Clark Pkwy
Percy St
Spring St
Amherst St
Reid St
South St
Woolfe St
America St
Drake St
E Bay St
Ashe St
Bogard St
Rose La
Mary St
Judith St
Wragg Mall
Chapel St
Alexander St
Ashley Ave
Cannon St
St Philip St
Ann St
Elizabeth St
Charlotte St
Morris St
John St
Radcliffe St
Hutson St
Calhoun St
Warren St
Thomas St
Vanderhorst St
Bee St
17
0 500 m
0 0.25 miles

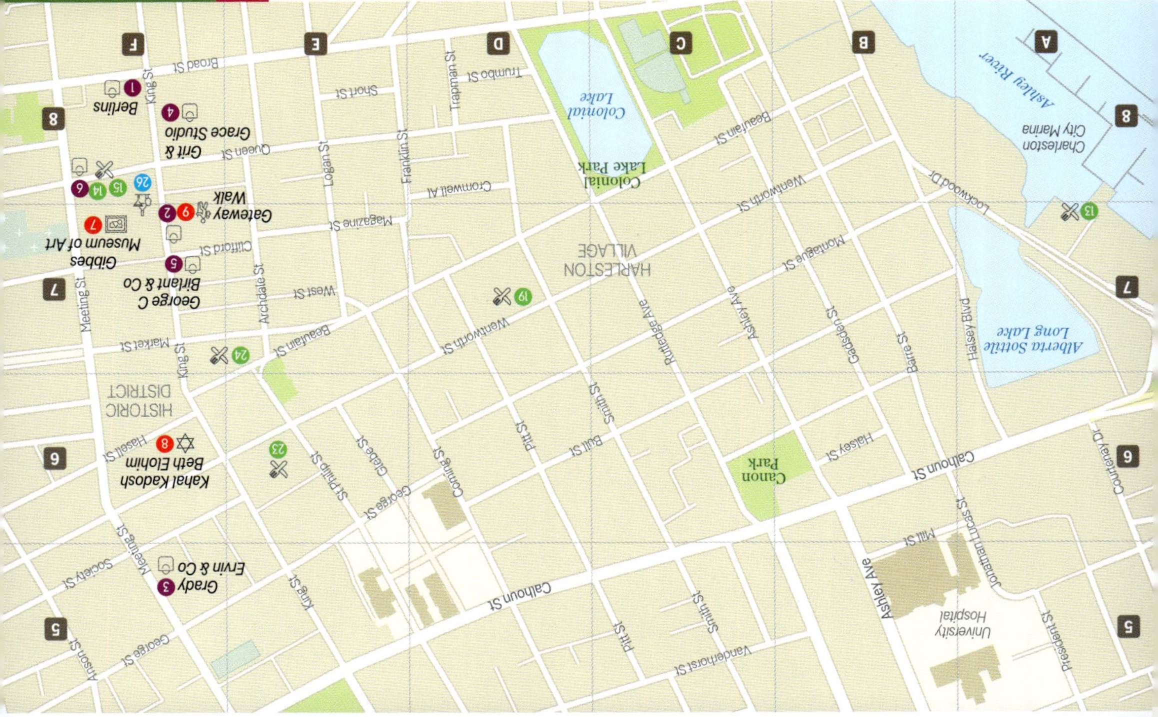

Berlins
Grit & Grace Studio
Gateway Walk
Gibbes Museum of Art
George C Birlant & Co
HISTORIC DISTRICT
Kahal Kadosh Beth Elohim
Grady Ervin & Co
HARLESTON VILLAGE
Colonial Lake Park
Colonial Lake
Canon Park
Alberta Sottile Long Lake
Ashley River
Charleston City Marina
University Hospital
Broad St
King St
Meeting St
Queen St
Clifford St
Market St
Archdale St
Hasell St
Magazine St
West St
Beaufain St
Logan St
Short St
Franklin St
Trapman St
Trumbo St
Cromwell Al
Wentworth St
St Philip St
Glebe St
George St
Coming St
Pitt St
Bull St
Smith St
Rutledge Ave
Ashley Ave
Montague St
Gadsden St
Barre St
Halsey St
Halsey Blvd
Lockwood Dr
Calhoun St
Mill St
Jonathan Lucas St
President St
Courtenay Dr
Vanderhorst St
Society St
Anson St

WALKING TOUR

Walk King Street

King St is the city's most celebrated shopping corridor, with numerous chains but also boutique retailers you won't encounter elsewhere. Upper King is peppered with quaint shops and galleries. You'll find antique stores and classic clothing shops on Lower King (p76). Good eats and coffee are plentiful along the way.

START	END	LENGTH
Callie's Hot Little Biscuit	Preservation Society of Charleston shop	1 mile; 1 hour

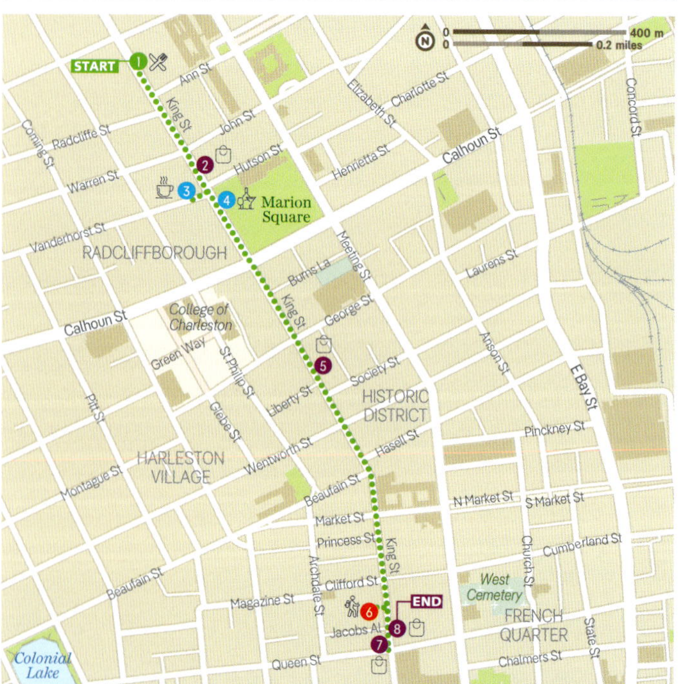

1 Hot Biscuits

Everyone raves about tiny **Callie's Hot Little Biscuit** on King St, and it's a real Charleston staple. Too many choices? Start with pimento cheese and country ham on a buttermilk biscuit.

2 Books New & Used

Pop into **Blue Bicycle Books**, an excellent new-and-used bookstore with a great selection covering Southern history and culture. The store hosts YALLfest, a young adult book festival, in November.

3 Coffee in the Yard

Caffeine up with an excellent espresso or relax with a craft beer – we're not judging – at welcoming **Kudu**, a cafe and beer bar just off Marion Sq. Students flow in and out from the nearby College of Charleston. Return to King St, passing Marion Sq.

4 Champagne & Grand Views

You can sip champagne at a pink marble bar beneath a dazzling chandelier – as one does – just steps from the lobby at stylishly grand **Hotel Bennett**. This locally owned hotel opened in 2019. Take a moment to admire the bright Charleston and Lowcountry mural that wraps around the first-floor rotunda. Cross King St.

5 Unique Jewelry

The name fits at cute **Croghan's Jewel Box**, a long-standing, family-owned jewelry store. It sells gorgeous antique pieces, estate finds, engagement rings and other one-of-a-kind gifts on Upper King.

6 Pass Through the Gate

There's an entry to the **Gateway Walk** on either side of King St south of Clifford St. This paved path leads to the eerie overgrown graveyard at the Unitarian Church or east to the courtyard at the Gibbes Museum.

7 More Books

Just steps from the Charleston Library, **Buxton Books** is a hub for book lovers, hosting regular author signings and book-release parties. Co-owner Julian Buxton leads walking tours spotlighting ghosts, Black history and the stories of Charleston.

8 Buy a Gift

If you're looking for a gift from your travels, even if just for yourself, you'll likely find something unique and locally made at the **Preservation Society of Charleston** (p76), with everything from cast-iron skillets from Smithey to cuffs and bow ties from Brackish.

EXPERIENCES

Shop for Southern Classics on Lower King Street SHOPPING

National retailers are muscling onto King St block by block, but a few bastions of all things pink, preppy and old-school hang tight on **Lower King** just north of Broad St. In fact, if you find yourself looking for a peacock-feather bow tie, Lower King has just the place.

Timeless elegance is the tagline at **Berlins** (MAP: 1 P72 **F8**; *berlinsclothing.com*), a clothing boutique for men and women open since 1883. Don't be put off by the slightly formal look of the place – the Southern hospitality here is instantly welcoming. Colorful dresses bring fashion-forward gals to **Beau & Ro** (MAP: 2 P72 **F7**; *beauandro.com*) to find a game-day frock, while dapper **Grady Ervin & Co** (MAP: 3 P72 **F5**; *gradyervin.com*) sells polo shirts, blazers and hunt-club jackets.

But quality apparel isn't the only draw. Painted oyster shells are a fun find at **Grit & Grace Studio** (MAP: 4 P72 **F8**; *gritandgracestudio.com*) – seek out the bright designs of Jonathan Green. Up the street, **George C Birlant & Co** (MAP: 5 P72 **F7**; *birlantantiquescharleston.com*) has been selling fine antiques for more than 100 years. And the peacock bow ties? Made by locally owned Brackish, they sit smartly on the shelves of the **Preservation Society of Charleston** (MAP: 6 P72 **F8**; *preservationsociety.org*), which sells unique products by local artists and creators.

Wander the Gibbes Museum of Art MUSEUM

MAP: 7 P72 **F7**

Squinting at the miniature portraits on the 2nd floor of the **Gibbes Museum of Art** *(gibbesmuseum.org; adult/child $12/6)* is an unexpected pleasure. Today, images of loved ones flood social media feeds, but Colonial-era travelers and soldiers had to make do with tiny painted portraits. Elsewhere in the museum, galleries display 18th- and 19th-century paintings, with plenty of eye-catching landscapes and formal portraits – you'll feel well versed in the grand families of historic Charleston! The contemporary collection includes works by local artists, with Lowcountry life a highlight. Don't miss sculptor Patrick Dougherty's soaring twig-and-branch installation Betwixt & Between in the 2nd-floor atrium.

The museum is a pleasant stop for an hour if you're strolling the Gateway Walk or exploring the nearby Historic District.

Embrace the Gothic on the Gateway Walk WALK

MAP: 9 P72 **F7**

If you're a fan of spooky Southern Gothic fiction, welcome to your unhappy place. This loose, natural-feeling **corridor** ribbons through downtown's hustle and bustle, but the weathered headstones, walled pathways and live oaks are an instant portal to another, quieter place. The silence is occasionally broken by church bells ringing in the distance. Defying the melancholy? Wildflowers, which deliver bursts of color in spring.

Established by the **Garden Club of Charleston** *(thegardenclubofcharleston.org)* in 1930 to celebrate the 250th anniversary of the city, the path was named for its many wrought-iron gates – which may be closed if you visit too early or late in the day. The path is under a half-mile one way. You'll find a basic map of the path on the garden club website.

The western entry is on Archdale St at **St John's Lutheran Church**. If the gate is closed, begin next door at the **Unitarian Church**. A memorial to the enslaved workers who built the church rises near the entrance. The path winds through the church graveyard and its overgrown foliage – and it's meant to grow wild like this. The walk passes the **Charleston Library** and the **Gibbes Museum of Art**. Next up is the progressive **Circular Congregational Church**, where the graveyard dates to 1695. Read more about its gravestone art at circularchurch.org. Conclude at **St Philip's Episcopal**.

JEWISH HERITAGE

MAP: 8 P72 **F6**

In the heart of Charleston, **Kahal Kadosh Beth Elohim** *(kkbe.org; tours adult/child $12/5)* is the oldest continuously used synagogue in the country, and the birthplace of the American Reform Judaism movement. Visitors can explore a museum and gift shop. Tours visit the recently renovated sanctuary; check the website for tour times. No tours Wednesday or Saturday. The synagogue also leads tours of Coming Street Cemetery, the oldest still surviving cemetery in the South.

Wander the Charleston Farmers Market

EVENTS AT MARION SQUARE

MAP: 10 P72 **E4**

Charleston's most frequented **park** is nearly 10 acres of green space in the middle of downtown, bordered by King, Calhoun, Meeting and Tobacco Sts. It's the home of a wildly popular **farmers market** *(8am-2pm Sat Apr-Nov)*, which supports Lowcountry farmers and growers. In December the market's hours are extended for the **Holiday Market**, which runs Saturdays and Sundays from 9am to 3pm. There's an annual Christmas-tree lighting in the park in early December.

First-year cadets at the Citadel (p64), known as knobs, march from campus to the park – which

CONTROVERSIAL STATUES

Marion Park's most iconic statue for 100 years was a soaring 115ft-high monument honoring South Carolinian John C Calhoun. It was taken down in 2020 as symbols of the Confederacy were removed across the South after the murder of George Floyd. Calhoun was the vice-president of the US from 1825 to 1832 and a passionate proponent of slavery.

was the first location of the school – on Recognition Day in March. This is the day knobs are welcomed into the full corps. The park also hosts an art exhibition during the **Spoleto Festival USA**, a citywide arts festival that kicks off in late May. Marion Sq is also a favored site for protest gatherings.

Sample Beer on the Charleston Brews Cruise — TOUR

MAP: 11 P72 **E3**

You can walk or ride a bus to several of the city's best breweries with the **Charleston Brews Cruise** *(brewscruise.com/charleston)*. Tours run buses to a rotating selection of three local breweries every day of the week. It also has a **happy-hour tour** *(per person $60)* at 5:15pm on Friday and Saturday with stops at just two breweries. Breweries currently in rotation are Holy City, Edmund's Oast, Frothy Beard, Common House, Palmetto and BrewLab.

Appreciate Art at the George Gallery — GALLERY

MAP: 12 P72 **B2**

A neighborhood favorite, this contemporary-art **gallery** displays mostly abstract and nonobjective work by artists from the East Coast with some connection to Charleston. There are no actual rules, though – just whatever the owner feels like. Check the website for opening receptions, held about once a month.

Campus Explorations — COLLEGE OF CHARLESTON

The University of Charleston website claims that students 'Live Life in a Postcard', and they are not exaggerating. *Travel + Leisure* named the campus at **College of Charleston** to be America's most beautiful in 2017.

Spread over a few city blocks at the center of Charleston's downtown, the campus is notable for its lush landscaping, which includes live oaks draped in Spanish moss, as well as its historic mansions and homes, some of which contain residence halls and Greek institutions. A public university founded in 1770, it is the oldest college in the state. It enrolls 11,700 students across undergraduate and graduate programs.

You can pick up a self-guided walking tour map at the Admissions Office (65 George St). Self-guided tours start at the pretty **Cistern Yard** in front of Randolph Hall. Now filled with dirt and covered

The Cistern Yard, College of Charleston
DEBBIE H PERKINS PHOTOGRAPHY/GETTY IMAGES ©

by a grassy lawn, the 1858 cistern could hold 40,000 gallons of water.

Pedestrians Rule the Street

2ND SUNDAY ON KING ST

If you're a shopper and want to mingle with the masses, time your visit to Charleston for the **2nd Sunday on King Street** *(charlestoncvb.com)*. That's when the city closes King St to cars, and locals descend on foot for shopping, eating and merriment. The closure begins at Calhoun St, which runs along the southern border of Marion Sq, and stretches south to Queen St. Food vendors, sidewalk musicians and selected artists add to the fun. King St is closed from noon until 5pm.

A HOLY CITY OF TOLERANCE

The New World was mostly populated by colonies founded by religious sects. Charleston was not among them. The 'Holy City,' as it came to be known for its numerous houses of worship, was instead a haven for religious tolerance, welcoming Anglicans, Anabaptists, French Huguenots, Quakers, Presbyterians, Congregationalists, Jews, and disciples of the Flying Spaghetti Monster. In fact, it was illegal in the colony to argue about religion. Today more than 400 houses of worship call Charleston home, and the skyline is defined by its steeples and spires. The law here dictates that no building can be higher than the tallest church steeple.

LISTINGS

Best Places for...

$ Budget $$ Midrange $$$ Top End

See p72 for map of locations

Eating

Southern US

Marina Variety Store $

13 A7

A long-standing, down-home, greasy-spoon kinda place, with harbor views and Southern hospitality as warm as the buttermilk biscuits. *7am-9pm Wed-Sat, to 2pm Sun*

Poogan's Porch $$

14 F8

The homemade butter-milk biscuits are out of control and the chicken and waffles are second to none. Boozy brunchers have plenty of options. *9am-3pm & 4:30-9:30pm*

Husk $$$

15 F8

The creation of acclaimed chef Sean Brock, Husk was one of the South's most buzzed-about restaurants. Brock has departed and so has a bit of the buzz, but the ingredients are local and the menu changes daily. *5-10pm daily, plus 10am-2pm Sat & Sun*

Seafood

Ordinary $$

16 D2

Inside a cavernous 1927 bank building, this lively seafood hall and oyster bar feels like the best party in town. The menu is short, but the delicious seafood is prepared with finesse. *5-10:30pm Wed-Mon*

Darling Oyster Bar $$

17 D3

Its light, flavorful oysters originate in places like Prince Edward Island and arrive at the table with a mild ginger mignon-ette. The Creole shrimp channels N'awlins and kills it. *4pm-2am Mon-Sat, 11am-2am Sun*

Fine Dining

Chez Nous $$

18 C3

A diminutive neighbor-hood restaurant with a tiny, nearly illegible short menu of dishes and wines hailing from southern France, northern Italy and northern Spain. *11:30am-3pm & 5-10pm*

Circa 1886 $$$

19 D7

In an elegant renovated carriage house at the Wentworth Mansion, this is Lowcountry fine dining at its most rewarding, with healthful seasonal offerings reflecting regional bounty and building on its traditions. *5-9pm Mon, Tue & Thu-Sat*

Halls Chophouse $$$

20 D4

Hands down the best restaurant for getting all done up, squeezing in at the bar and ordering a sizable, rare cut of steak with several glasses of Napa Valley cabernet. *4-11pm Mon-Thu, to mid-night Fri, 11am to midnight Sat, 10am-11pm Sat*

Affordable Eats

Pass $

21 C2

The piled-high gourmet sandwiches draw College of Charleston students by the golf-cart load. One roast-beef option gives a tasty nod to the famous sandwich showcased in HBO's *The Bear*. *10am-3pm Wed-Sat*

Xiao Bao Biscuit $

22 B3

Casual but stylish eatery with a delicious, palate-kicking menu of simple pan-Asian fare enhanced by local ingredients and spicy flavors. Try the *okonomiyaki* – a Japanese cabbage pancake – with egg and bacon. *11am-10pm Mon-Sat*

Health Food

Basic Kitchen $$

23 E6

With dishes like avo toast, fresh sesame kale and rainbow bowls, this healthy and delicious little cafe feels like something you'd stumble across in Bali. Vegetarians are well served here. *11am-3pm & 5-9pm Mon-Fri, 10am-3pm & 5-9pm Sat & Sun*

Italian

Le Farfalle $$$

24 E7

Seafood charcuterie doesn't get better than the octopus carpaccio at Le Farfalle, a breath of fresh Tuscan air with a bright, spacious dining room and cheeky yet sophisticated waitstaff. *5-9:30pm Sun-Tue, to 10pm Thu-Sat*

Drinking

Wine Bars

Camellias

25 E4

Sip champagne beneath a sparkling chandelier at Camellias, the very pink bar inside the Hotel Bennett that's designed to look like a Fabergé egg. Also serves a reservation-required afternoon tea service. *4-10pm Mon-Thu, 5pm-midnight Fri & Sat*

Bin 152

26 F8

Pair the adventurous wine selections with imported cheese, freshly baked bread and other charcuterie bits at this elegant downtown wine bar. *2pm-midnight Mon-Thu, noon-midnight Fri-Sun*

Cocktails

Prohibition

27 D3

This delightful Jazz Age gastropub serves up excellent craft cocktails (from $16) that tend to pair well with the lip-smackin' Southern grub. *4pm-2am Mon-Thu, 11am-2am Fri-Sun*

100 Proof

28 D4

It may be snug, but the cocktails are first class – the mixologist is some kind of visionary. *noon-2am Thu-Sun, 4pm-2am Mon-Wed*

Distillery

High Wire Distilling

29 C1

At this bright tasting room you take shots of small-batch gin, whiskey, bourbon and amaro ($14). Tours ($10) and tasty cocktails are also available. *10am-6pm Mon-Sat, to 2pm Sun*

See p96
for eating
and drinking
listings

Explore
Charleston County Sea Islands

Make time for the sea islands, known for their wildly scenic marshes and broad beaches. There are a dozen in Charleston County within an hour's drive of the city. Sullivan's Island and Isle of Palms beckon day-trippers for lazy beach days. They are 10 miles by road southeast of Charleston on the Mount Pleasant side. Four miles in the other direction is James Island, one of the more urban barrier sea islands. Beyond James Island, Folly Beach is good for a day of sun and sand. Further south you'll find Kiawah, a swanky resort town with a gorgeous beach, and Edisto Island (ed-is-tow), home to wild Lowcountry bliss.

Getting Around

Car

Traffic is increasing across the sea islands, but driving is the most practical way to explore. Byways and bridges link the islands, but you won't always find a direct connection between them. Kiawah and Edisto are the farthest from the city.

Bus

Bus travel from Charleston to the islands is typically not time efficient or practical. From June through August, however, consider the Beach Reach Shuttle from Mount Pleasant town center to traffic-congested Isle of Palms County Beach.

THE BEST

GUIDED TOUR McLeod Plantation (p86)

OUTDOOR ADVENTURE Exploring Botany Bay (p86)

MEAL WITH A VIEW Bowens Island Restaurant (p94)

LIVE MUSIC Pour House (p94)

BREWERY Low Tide (p97)

Edisto Island (p90)
ALISHA BUBE/SHUTTERSTOCK ©

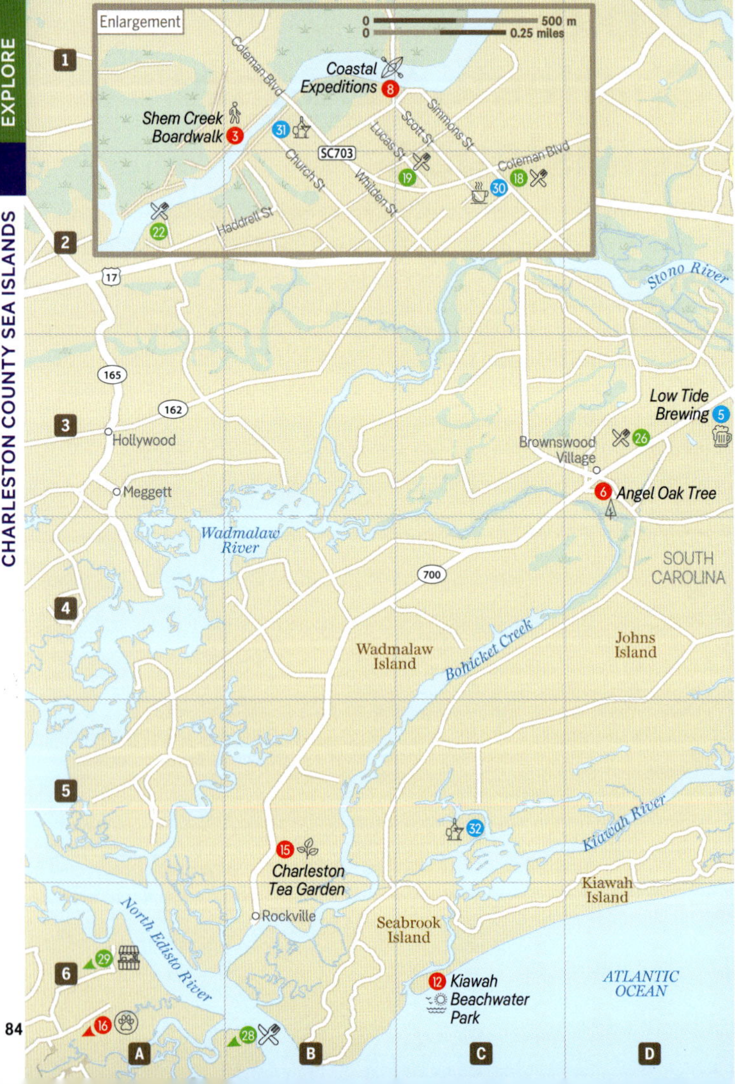
A
B
C
D
1
2
3
4
5
6
Enlargement
0 500 m
0 0.25 miles
Coastal Expeditions 8
Shem Creek Boardwalk 3
31
Coleman Blvd
Simmons St
Scott St
Lucas St
SC703
Church St
Whilden St
19
30
18
Coleman Blvd
22
Haddrell St
17
Stono River
165
162
Hollywood
Meggett
Low Tide Brewing 5
26
Brownswood Village
6 Angel Oak Tree
Wadmalaw River
700
SOUTH CAROLINA
Bohicket Creek
Wadmalaw Island
Johns Island
32
Kiawah River
15
Charleston Tea Garden
Rockville
Kiawah Island
Seabrook Island
North Edisto River
29
12 Kiawah Beachwater Park
ATLANTIC OCEAN
16
28

EXPLORE

CHARLESTON COUNTY SEA ISLANDS

★ TOP EXPERIENCE

McLeod Plantation

A grand oak alley frames the Victorian-style home that anchors the McLeod Plantation, but this striking facade doesn't match the reality. The upper-middle-class owners of this Sea Island cotton farm strived to keep pace with wealthier neighbors, and their enslaved workers were pushed to their limits. Tours deftly examine their experiences and mistreatment.

MAP P84 **F2**

PLANNING TIP
Guided tours add helpful context and interesting details; otherwise, enrich your experience by downloading the free *McLeod Plantation Historic Site* app.

Scan this QR code for prices and tour information.

McLeod Home

It's a short walk from the visitor center to the 19th-century Victorian-style **plantation home**, which isn't furnished or particularly grand. The ground floor contains what was once a formal parlor, a dining room and a small library with simple woodwork. A 1920s renovation reversed the orientation: the back door became the front entrance, and a small porch was replaced by a new portico with columns. An indoor kitchen was also installed.

While the house isn't much to see, the story of its unique series of occupants is nothing short of revelatory. They include the McLeod family, the Confederate army, the Union army, a federal agency that aimed to help the formerly enslaved transition to freedom, and the Charleston County Park & Recreation Commission.

Transition Row

A row of cramped, basic wooden cabins (pictured) near the house was originally built to house enslaved people, and until 1960 the cabins offered no electricity or running water (only one house ever

ANDREW MONTGOMERY/LONELY PLANET ©

included indoor plumbing). After the war, the cabins became transitional housing for formerly enslaved people who had been freed, and a look inside gives visitors considerable insight into how generations of Gullah families lived.

After the McLeods regained control of the property the cabins were rented out as family homes, often to the descendants of the enslaved, until the last McLeod's death in 1990.

Places of Worship

Over the years a couple of different structures served as places of worship on the McLeod Plantation. In one of the old barns, a minister who was paid by Mr McLeod preached to African Americans about how they were to serve God by obediently performing their duties on the plantation.

QUICK BREAK
Dig into the fried grouper plate at marsh-front **Ellis Creek Fish Camp** *(elliscreekfishcamp.com)*, 2 miles from the McLeod Plantation.

DESCENDENTS
One of the descendants of a formerly enslaved worker on the plantation became a caretaker for the grandson of the man who had owned her great-great-grandparents.

The property also contains a former cabin for the enslaved that was converted into a worship house in the 1970s. From here, the Children of God Mission regaled James Island residents with gospel music via transistor radio.

Gullah Cemetery

You can also visit what may be the most telling site on the plantation grounds: a wooded area that doubles as a Gullah cemetery, where more than 100 people are anonymously buried. The remains of children are contained in 42 of the graves, a testament to the brutal conditions on the plantation. Gullah people believed in an afterlife in which they rejoined their African ancestors.

NEALA MCCARTEN/ALAMY STOCK PHOTO ©

Occupants of the McLeod Plantation

The McLeod plantation home (pictured) was built by the labor of enslaved people just before the Civil War, and its first owner, William Wallace McLeod, also ordered a fence constructed around the house to separate his family space from the homes of the enslaved.

During the Civil War, the McLeod family (and all island residents) evacuated, and the plantation was occupied by Confederate soldiers. In 1865 the Union army captured the island and made the McLeod Plantation their headquarters, then turned it over to the Bureau for Refugees, Freedmen and Abandoned Lands, a government agency that helped transition four million formerly enslaved people to freedom. The home briefly served as a school for freed children and as a medical treatment facility. Parcels of the land were doled out to the formerly enslaved.

In 1868 the political climate changed, the agency helping the formerly enslaved closed and the McLeod family clawed back the property. For the next 100 years the family maintained control over a workforce of the formerly enslaved that lived and toiled in much the same conditions as they had before the war. Laws were passed that resembled the old slave code, punishments were more severe than in a free-labor society, and the dream of land ownership receded as payment for labor came in food rations and a portion of the harvest.

Plantation Today

The last member of the McLeod family died in 1990 and left instructions in a will for the plantation to be preserved. Today it is managed by the Charleston County Park & Recreation Commission.

GUIDED TOURS
The 45-minute guided tour starts behind the **visitor center** *(9:30am, 10:30am, 12:30pm, 1:30pm & 2:30pm)*. See the website for up-to-date tour times.

WILLIAM MCLEOD
The McLeods were strong supporters of the Confederacy, and William McLeod was part of a movement to secede from the Union 10 years before it actually happened.

Drive Botany Bay on Edisto Island

Sea breezes carry whispers of the past beneath live oaks and soaring pines at wild and weathered Botany Bay. Step from your car into this gorgeous tableau to admire a regal oak alley, eerie skeleton trees and the ruins of an old cotton plantation. Botany Bay is about 50 miles from Charleston. The area is closed on Tuesday.

START	END	LENGTH
Botany Bay Wildlife Management Area Info Kiosk	Botany Bay Wildlife Management Area Info Kiosk	6.5 miles

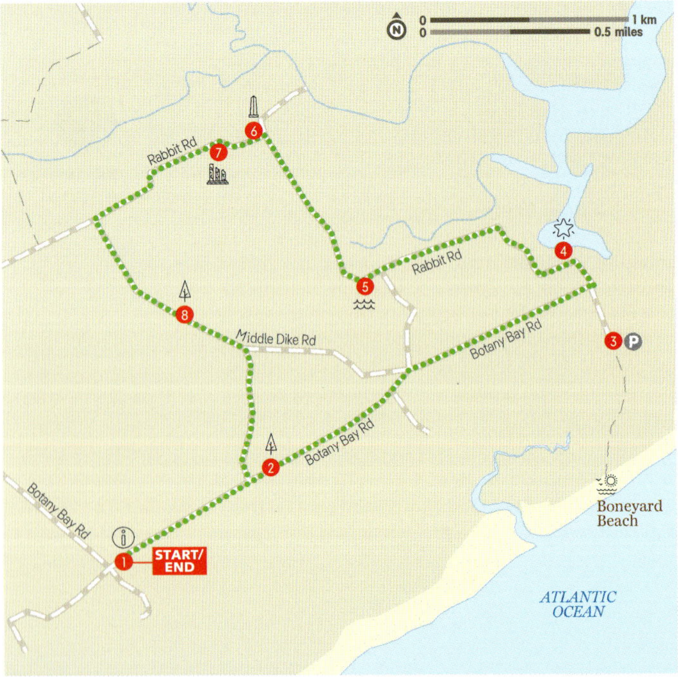

1 Information Kiosk

After a long drive down Botany Bay Rd, turn left into the wildlife management area. Stop at the **information kiosk** to fill out a free permit and pick up a driving tour map. Interpretative signs dot the road as it twists through this 3363-acre landscape.

2 Avenue of Oaks

A long **avenue of live oaks** provides shade and a portal to the past. This oak allée was the dramatic entranceway to the Bleak Hall cotton plantation, one of two plantations at Botany Bay before the Civil War.

3 Pockoy Island

Turn right at the T junction at the end of the road and drive to the parking area for **Pockoy Island**. The beach on this rapidly eroding sea island can only be reached via the half-mile, wheelchair-accessible trail from the parking area. It ends at Boneyard Beach, where fallen 'skeleton' trees set a moody scene. The beach can only be reached at low tide; tide times are posted at the start of the trail.

4 Bleak Hall Plantation

Return to the T junction and continue straight to the former grounds of **Bleak Hall cotton plantation**, which was in operation for 150 years. Today just a few 'tabby' outbuildings, made of oysters, lime and sand, remain. The road then passes Ocella Creek, where markers share details about the lives of the enslaved who worked the fields.

5 Picnic Pond

An oak tree overlooks a small **pond** on your left. The last private owners of Botany Bay loved this pretty spot, and today an engraved stone marker honors their care for the property. Look for frogs and wood ducks. From here, the road crosses Ocella Creek.

6 Enslaved Workers Memorial

A **marker** lists the names of the men, women and children who were enslaved at the Bleak Hall and Sea Cloud plantations between 1740 and 1865.

7 Manor Ruins

The overgrown **ruins** of the manor house anchoring Sea Cloud Plantation rise on your left. Rice and Sea Island cotton were cultivated on the surrounding grounds. As you continue, look for a beehive-shaped brick well.

8 Pine-Hardwood Forest

The last leg of the drive tunnels though a **lush corridor of green** formed by soaring pines, thick hardwoods and vibrant ferns. Managed today by the state, this feral landscape was once a clear-cut field used for cotton cultivation. End back at the information kiosk.

EXPERIENCES

Watch the Sunset from the Arthur Ravenel Jr Bridge BRIDGE

If you don't mind a bit of wind-swept walking, you can catch the sunset from an inspiring spot: the **Arthur J Ravenel Bridge** (MAP: 1 P84 G2). This graceful span over the Cooper River links the town of Mount Pleasant and the Charleston Historic District. The 2.5-mile **Wonders Way** is the pedestrian path over the cable-stayed bridge, which rises about 200ft above the river and provides gorgeous views of both communities. There's a parking lot at the **Mount Pleasant Waterfront Park** and the adjacent **Mount Pleasant Visitor Center & Sweetgrass Basket Pavilion** (MAP: 2 P84 G2) with access to the pedestrian path. The bridge opened in 2005.

The annual **Cooper River Bridge Run** in early April is a 10km footrace over the bridge that draws 38,500 runners and ends with a party in Marion Sq.

Kick Back Beside Shem Creek WATERFRONT

MAP: 3 P84 B1

Before sunset you can join the party along **Shem Creek** in Mount Pleasant, where folks drink beer on restaurant patios and soak up views of the creek and Charleston Harbor. You can stretch your legs and scan for dolphins along the dock-lined **Shem Creek Boardwalk**, which overlooks the marsh. Various boats and the occasional kayaker are also part of the backdrop. For an easy-going vibe after your walk, settle in with a beer on the deck at Red's Ice House (p97).

Walk the Pitt Street Bridge WALK

MAP: 4 P84 H2

You'll join dog walkers and likely an egret or two on a quiet stroll along the **Pitt Street Bridge** *(experiencemountpleasant.com)*, a paved pedestrian path tucked behind a residential neighborhood in Mount Pleasant. The first bridge here, a simple structure made of plank-topped barrels, was completed in 1777. It was the first span to connect Mount Pleasant with Sullivan's Island. Today, the palm-lined path ribbons above scenic marshes and ends at a small fishing pier. It's a pretty spot to stretch your legs and watch the sunset. Signage shares details about the birds you might see. To the pier and back is about 0.8 miles. Park on Pitt St near the bridge. For a post-walk fuel-up, stop at Brown Fox Coffee (p97) .

Pay Your Respects to the Angel Oak Tree on Johns Island HISTORIC SITE

MAP: 6 P84 D3

Anticipation builds on the bumpy, tree-lined drive to the **Angel Oak Tree** *(angeloaktree.com)*. And yes, this enormous Southern live oak and its many branches are an impressive payoff – some folks say the tree is 1500 years old (others says it's

400 to 500 years old). The drawback to a visit? With tourist buses and endless posted rules, this old-timer feels, well, diminished. The rules and signage are surely there to protect the tree, but they detract from the grandeur – and the perfect picture. Whatever the case, it's one of the oldest living organisms east of the Mississippi, standing 66.5ft tall and measuring 28ft around. Its thick branches shoot off in all directions, in many cases twisting to the ground and back up again. Although there's no climbing allowed, you can take tree selfies. Its hours are 9am to 5pm Monday through Saturday and 1pm to 5pm Sunday.

A small **gift shop** on the property contains tree art and various books, and about 15 signs forbidding visitors from reading the books without purchasing them. Don't even try it! The shop closes at 4:30pm.

Get out on the Water BOATING

Numerous companies lead tours and boat trips through the marshes and along the coasts of the sea islands. **Adventure Harbor Tours** (MAP: 7 P84 **F2**; *facebook.com/adventureharbortours*) runs harbor cruises, sunset excursions and fun trips to uninhabited Morris Island – great for shelling. Trips leave from the marina at Ashley Point in Charleston. Well-established **Coastal Expeditions** (MAP: 8 P84 **B1**; *coastalexpeditions.com; kayak tour adult/child from $48/38*) leads kayak tours through the salt marshes at Shem Creek and along the Kiawah River, where full-moon trips are on the schedule. Also rents kayaks.

Spend a Day on the Beach BEACH

There's a **county park** *(ccprc.com)* with restrooms, parking and seasonal amenities at each beach except Sullivan's Island. Parking costs $5 to $20.

Seven-mile **Isle of Palms** (MAP: 9 P84 **H2**) is well suited to families. Lifeguards watch the ocean in warmer months, and there's a playground. The parking lot fills quickly in summer.

EDGAR ALLAN POE

Poet and short story writer Edgar Allan Poe, known for his keen sense of the macabre, was stationed at **Fort Moultrie** from 1827 to 1828. The object of affection in the eerie poem *Annabel Lee*, one of his most famous, is rumored to have been buried in the graveyard at the **Unitarian Church** (p73) on Archdale St. You'll likely hear her story mentioned on a Charleston ghost tour. Ponder his poetry over a good burger at **Poe's Tavern** *(poestavern.com)* on Sullivan's Island not far from Fort Moultrie. 'It was many and many a year ago, in a kingdom by the sea...'

Commerce-free **Sullivan's Island** (MAP: 10 P84 **H2**) is a broad sweep of sand south of Mount Pleasant. Come here to avoid the crowds. Restaurants hug Middle St between Station 22 St and Station 22½ St. Parking is free on residential streets, but be sure all four wheels are off the road.

Festive **Folly Beach** (MAP: 11 P84 **F5**) feels the most like a beach town – it's the best for surfing and retains a bohemian vibe. Enjoy broad shores and a small but convivial oceanfront community anchored by Center St.

Kiawah Island is mostly private, but visitors can enjoy a wonderful beach day at family-friendly **Kiawah Beachwater Park** (MAP: 12 P84 **C6**), which has seasonal lifeguards, beach-chair rentals and refreshments.

Enjoy Yoga, Fresh Produce & the Dead at the Pour House

LIVE MUSIC

MAP: 13 P84 **E2**

The murals are vivid at the **Pour House** *(charlestonpourhouse.com)* on James Island, where you can commune with fellow Deadheads every Wednesday night starting at 7pm. The popular show, by the Reckoning tribute band, is one of many weekly events at this indoor-outdoor concert venue, which has become an unexpected community hub. The **Sunday Brunch Farmers Market** is a boozy brunch that coincides with the vendor-filled market, which runs from 10am to 3pm in the parking lot. Before the market opens you can join a **yoga class** *(evolvemobilemovement.com; $10)* on the back deck on Sunday mornings at 9:30am. The building is also home to buzzy Kwei Fei (p97). Stop by the Pour House anytime to view the many murals, which change regularly thanks to an annual competition.

Devour Oysters on Bowens Island

SEAFOOD

MAP: 14 P84 **F4**

Grab your beer and loads of napkins, then find a seat on the deck overlooking the quiet marshlands. This fine scene will soon be improved by the oysters coming your way. Down a long dirt road through Lowcountry seagrasses near Folly Beach, this unpainted wooden **shack** *(bowensisland.com; 11am-9:30pm Tue-Sat)* is

NIGHTLIFE

Folly Beach is the best (and edgiest) for nightlife, with a few bars in the island's center by the Tides Hotel and along Center St. Sullivan's Island skews yuppie and has great people-watching. **Isle of Palms** has a good scene as well, particularly in the summer. There are a few good craft breweries on Johns Island, including **Low Tide Brewing** (MAP: 5 P84 **D3**; *lowtidebrewing.com*).

one of the South's most venerable seafood dives – grab an oyster knife and start shucking! Cool beer and friendly locals give the place its soul. Also well worth a try is the hefty Lowcountry boil, a messy celebration of shrimp, sausage, potatoes and corn on the cob. It's also known as Frogmore stew. The restaurant has been here since 1946, the magical sunsets even longer.

Explore a Tea Plantation on Wadmalaw Island PLANTATION

MAP: 15 P84 **B5**

Hop on the trolley and learn fun facts about tea at the **Charleston Tea Garden** *(charlestonteagarden.com)*, the only large-scale working tea plantation in the US. The **trolley tour** *(adult/child $18/9.50)* will take you around the property, and it offers plenty of information on the history and process of growing tea plants. A free tour of the production facility gives insight into the magic behind green, oolong and black tea, which are all – perhaps surprisingly – sourced from the leaves of the same plant, *camellia sinensis*. It's the processing that changes the taste.

The **gift shop** has lots of goodies and souvenirs, including free bottomless hot and cold tea. The garden is 22 miles from downtown Charleston.

Give a Side Eye to Snakes at Edisto Island Serpentarium ZOO

MAP: 16 P84 **A6**

If you're afraid of snakes, perhaps don't come here. Everyone else? This place is pretty cool. Around 50 years of reptile obsession by owners Ted and Heyward Clamp culminate in this **serpentarium** *(edistoserpentarium.com; adult/child $20/15)*, which differs from most in that you can see snakes living in their natural habitats, separated from visitors by low-walled enclosures rather than glass. Alligators, lizards, turtles and crocodiles also call the outdoor serpentarium home. Think of it as a reptilian Disneyland.

Take a Polar Plunge in Folly Beach EVENT

MAP: 17 P84 **F5**

Dress up like greenskeeper Carl Spackler and jump into the ocean on the first day of the year during the **Bill Murray Look-a-Like Polar Plunge** *(visitfolly.com)*. This subzero swim pays homage to Charleston's most distinguished resident, Bill Murray, with participants attempting to resemble him in various roles. Everyone is encouraged to 'freeze your bills off,' and prizes are given for the best costumes.

LISTINGS

See p84 for map of locations

Best Places for...

$ Budget $$ Midrange $$$ Top End

Eating

Mount Pleasant

Mount Pleasant Farmers Market $
18 C2
Forty local vendors and farmers (but no artisans, jewelers or anyone else non-food-related) sell produce, seafood, baked goods and freshly prepared meals. *3:30-7pm Tue Apr-Sep*

Page's Okra Grill $
 C2
Cars pull up early for Southern breakfasts, like buttermilk biscuits slathered in sausage gravy, and Lowcountry crabcakes with Cajun remoulade. Cocktails too. *7am-9pm Mon-Thu, 7am-11 Fri, 8am-10pm Sat, 8am-3pm Sun*

Five Loaves Cafe $
 H1
Eco-minded cafe serving salads and gourmet sandwiches. The delicious daily soups earn raves. *11am-9pm Mon-Sat, 10am-3pm & 5-8pm Sun*

Grace & Grit $$
 G2
Try a grit flight at brunch or dinner at this stylish restaurant serving fresh seafood with a Southern spin. *5-9pm Tue-Thu, to 9:30pm Fri, 9:30am-2pm & 5-9pm Sat, 9:30am-2:30pm & 5-9:30pm Sun*

Wreck of the Richard & Charlene $$$
 A2
Shem Creek's best seafood shack serves up heaping paper plates of shrimp, scallops, fish, oysters, deviled crab and stone crab. Fried, boiled or grilled. *5-8:30pm Tue-Sat*

Sullivan's Island

Poe's Tavern $
23 H2
On a sunny day the front porch of Poe's on Sullivan's Island is the place to be. The tavern's namesake, Edgar Allan Poe, was once stationed at nearby Fort Moultrie. Try the burgers. *11am-10pm*

High Thyme $$
 H2
Stop into this chic cottage for seafood and steaks prepared with tasty twists on Southern favorites. *5-10pm Mon-Sat*

Home Team BBQ $$
see  H2
This is the Sullivan's Island outpost of the Charleston-area chain known for its pulled pork. Try the carnitas tacos. Craft beer and cocktails too. *11am-midnight*

Obstinate Daughter $$
 H3
Dig into light and playful plates of fresh veggies, pasta, seafood and unusual ingredients at this regional top choice. Raw oysters are flown in from top locales. Vegetarians will leave exuberant. Welcoming staff complete the experience. *11am-10pm Mon-Fri, 10am-10pm Fri & Sat*

Johns Island & Folly Beach

Tattooed Moose $
 D3
Refreshingly exotic sandwiches including a Lowcountry Cuban, a Moroccan gyro and the wildly popular Lucky

#1 (with pork belly and kimchi). Locations on Johns Island and in NoMo. *11:30am-2am*

Chico Feo $

 F4

Tacos are small and messy but totally excellent at this laid-back Folly Beach favorite serving a range of international dishes, plus wine and beer. *11am-2am*

Kwei Fe $$

see 13 E2

Sharing a building with the Pour House on Johns Island, this Szechuan joint serves fiery snacks and dishes. *5-9pm Tue-Thu, to 10pm Fri & Sat*

Wild Olive $$

see 5 D3

Cozy Italian kitchen on Johns Island whipping up some of the best homemade pastas and ambitious mains outside of Tuscany. *5-10pm Mon-Thu, 4-11pm Fri & Sat, 4-10pm Sun*

Edisto Island

Whaley's Store $

 B6

Want local flavor? Then pull into this former gas station where pick-up trucks are lined up like horses out front. Enjoy smash burgers, fried seafood baskets and cold beer. *11:30am-9pm Mon, Tue, Fri & Sat, to 10pm Wed, Thu & Sun*

King's Farm Market $

 A6

Pause along the highway for fresh produce, local jams and jellies, macadamia-nut cookies, key lime pie, jalapeño-pimento cheese and a friendly hello. *9:30am-5:30pm Mon-Sat, to 5pm Sun*

Drinking

Mount Pleasant

Brown Fox Coffee

30 C2

Crowds queue up early for Foxy Chais and Raspberry White Mochas at this low-slung coffee joint. *7am-4pm Mon-Fri, 8am-3pm Sat*

Red's Ice House

 B1

Sip beer by Shem Creek while admiring the many boats. *11am-10pm Sun-Thu, to 11pm Fri & Sat*

Johns Island & Folly Beach

Low Tide Brewing

see 5 D3

A friendly neighborhood brewery on Johns Island with 12 taps spouting solid craft beers. Try the Romance in the Dark, a dark sour with a hint of cherry flavor. Solo travelers will feel welcome. *3-10pm Mon-Thu, noon-midnight Fri & Sat, noon-10pm Sun*

Jack of Cups

see  F4

This Folly Beach watering hole looks like your average neighborhood pub, with a sunny back patio to boot. But the from-scratch menu, which changes daily, sets it apart. *11:30am-10pm Wed-Mon*

Linnette's

32 C5

The chattering classes are abuzz about this dapper number at the Dunlin, a brand new Auberge property on Johns Island, named for a shorebird. Come for cocktails like The Wildcat Cup, with moonshine and smoked pecan. *11am-10pm Sun-Thu, to 11pm Fri & Sat*

See p111
for eating
and drinking
listings

Explore
Beaufort & Hilton Head

The southern half of the South Carolina coast is a tangle of islands cut off from the mainland by inlets and tidal marshes. Here, descendants of enslaved West Africans known as the Gullah maintain small communities. On Port Royal Island, colonial Beaufort (byoo-furt) is the second-oldest city in South Carolina, and a prominent educator on the post–Civil War period. The streets are lined with 18th-century mansions and twisting magnolias. Across Port Royal Sound, Hilton Head Island is South Carolina's largest barrier island and one of America's top golf spots. One of the first eco-planned destinations in the US, it has 12 miles of continuous beachfront.

Getting Around

Car

Most people explore the Lowcountry by car. Traffic is heavy in Beaufort and Hilton Head, particularly at rush hour and on weekends. If you're staying in Sea Pines or the southern end of Hilton Head, take the 6-mile Cross Island Parkway to avoid congestion. There's a $9 day-pass vehicle fee to enter the Sea Pines Resort area.

Bicycle

Bike trails and multiuse pathways crisscross the island, and in places you can pedal on the beach at low tide. You'll have to pay an entrance fee to cycle in the Sea Pines Resort.

THE BEST

HISTORIC EXPERIENCE Reconstruction Era National Historical Park (p102)

DAY TRIP Daufuskie Island (p106)

TOUR Pat Conroy's Beaufort Tour (p108)

CAMPGROUND Hunting Island State Park (p109)

COCKTAIL WITH A VIEW Quarterdeck (p111)

Hilton Head Island (p109)

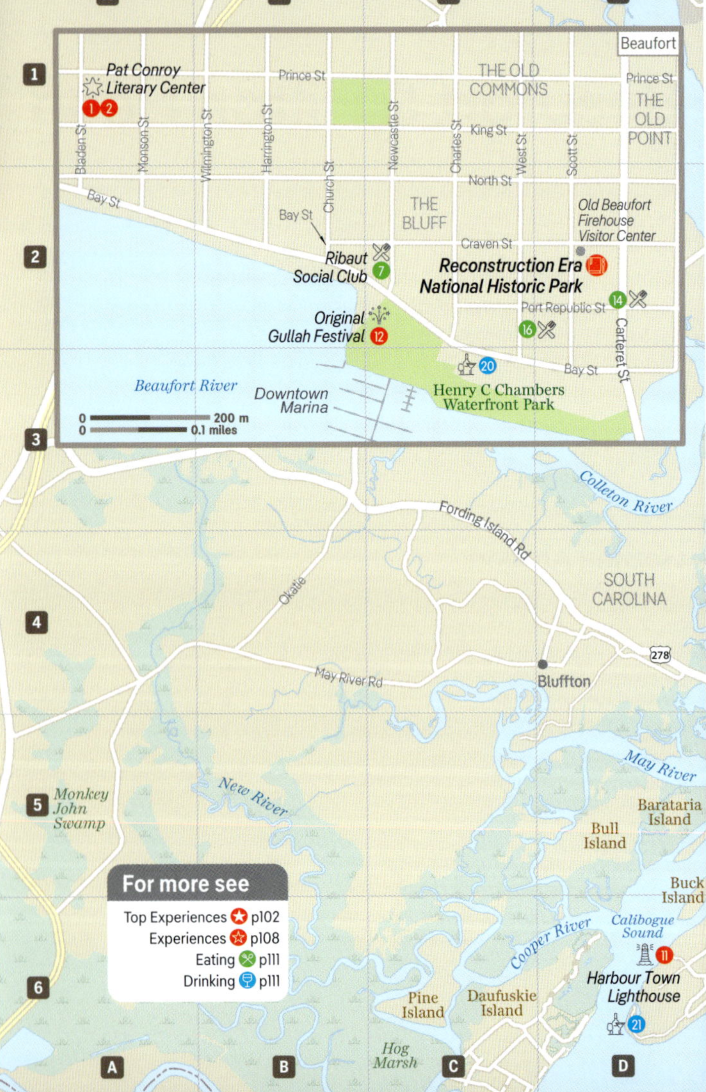

For more see
Top Experiences p102
Experiences p108
Eating p111
Drinking p111

E
F
G
H
0
10 km
0
5 miles
1
2
3
4
5
6
See Beaufort Enlargement
Carolina Cider Company & Superior Coffee
21
See St Helena Island Enlargement
Pinckney-Porter's Chapel
Camp Saxton
Shell Point
Port Royal
Broad River
St Helena Island
Lands End Rd
Seaside Rd
Parris Island Museum
Parris Island
Chechessee River
Hunting Island
Corn Island
Port Royal Sound
Big Harry Island
Pinckney Island
Hilton Head Island
St Helena Island
Brick Baptist Church
Frances Butler La
Coastal Discovery Museum
Native Son Adventures
Dr Martin Luther King Jr Dr
Penn Center
Broad Creek
278
Jazz Corner
Darrah Hall
Holland Ct
ATLANTIC OCEAN
Gullah-N-Geechie Mahn Tours
0
100 m

★ TOP EXPERIENCE

Reconstruction Era National Historic Park

From 1861 to 1900 Beaufort and the surrounding sea islands became a hub for organization, education and self-determination for the formerly enslaved, who comprised 80% of the local population. Established by Congress in 2019, the Reconstruction Era National Historic Park *(nps.gov/reer)* showcases the history of this era at three separate sites.

MAP P100 **D2**

PLANNING TIP
Tour one of the park's three sites to best learn the region's history. Confirm times the day before.

Scan this QR code for further information.

Getting Started

The best way to experience this new national historic park is by listening to the stories shared by rangers and docents and recounted in videos. This evolving collection of sites and exhibits – located in Beaufort and Port Royal and on St Helena Island – explores the experiences of Black Americans in Beaufort and the surrounding Lowcountry during and after the Civil War. Currently, many exhibits are text heavy, but ranger talks, guided tours and on-site videos add vibrancy to the history. To ensure the best experience, check the online calendar before you visit to confirm that you can join a tour.

Admission to the park is free, although there is a $15 fee for a self-guided tour of the small Penn Center museum, which is managed separately. If a docent is available at the Penn Center, you can join a $20 docent-led tour.

Old Beaufort Firehouse Visitor Center

The best starting point is the **Old Beaufort Firehouse Visitor Center** in downtown Beaufort. In this compact space you'll find a few exhibits as well

DEBORAH MCCAGUE/SHUTTERSTOCK ©

as details about the other sites and scheduled park programs. Guided walking tours currently depart the visitor center at 11am and 2pm Tuesday through Saturday.

Reconstruction Era History

In November 1861, Union forces prevailed in the Battle of Port Royal, laying siege to Confederate forts on Hilton Head Island and St Helena Island. When owners of enslaved people in Beaufort caught wind of this, they all skipped town in what a newspaper columnist famously dubbed Beaufort's 'Great Skedaddle.'

As tour guides tell it, white citizens left so fast that Union soldiers found half-eaten suppers on the tables. There was fear of a revolt, because back then Beaufort's population was 80% enslaved people. These newly freed African Americans were left behind to tend to the homes – such

QUICK BREAK
Pop into **Carolina Cider Company & Superior Coffee** *(carolinaciderco.com)* for coffee, cider, pastries and loads of jams and jellies. This cozy building is on the Sea Island Parkway 3 miles from Darrah Hall.

COME HEAR THE NEWS
The 33rd United States Colored Troops listened to a public reading of Abraham Lincoln's Emancipation Proclamation at Camp Saxton on January 1, 1863.

as Cuthbert House (pictured, p103) – all of which remain standing today. For this reason, Beaufort is an exceptional place to visit not only to view magnificent antebellum houses but also to learn about the Reconstruction Era and the culture of the Gullah people, who are descendants of the formerly enslaved.

After the war, Beaufort's infrastructure was largely converted into hospitals where soldiers and the formerly enslaved got medical care. Over on St Helena Island, Penn School was established to educate the formerly enslaved and provide social services and employment assistance.

Camp Saxton

At Camp Saxton in nearby Port Royal, 5000 African Americans (many of whom were enslaved)

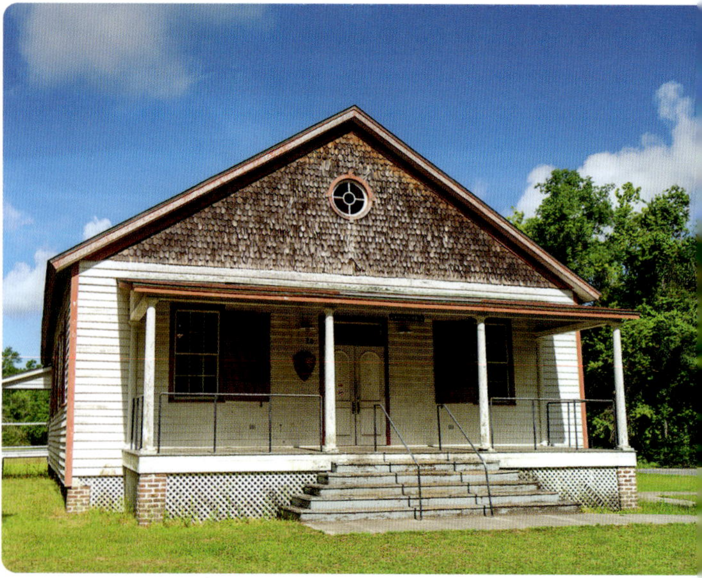

were recruited to join the Union army. Guided tours of the camp currently depart the **Pinckney-Porter's Chapel visitor center** on Saturday at noon.

Penn Center National Historic Landmark District

The **Penn Center** (p108) was the home of one of the nation's first schools for the formerly enslaved, and today it sits within a small complex of buildings on St Helena Island. The national park service runs one building here, **Darrah Hall** (pictured), which was a longtime community hub and recreation center. Built in the 1890s, it is the oldest standing structure on the school grounds.

You'll find exhibits inside, and tours are currently offered at 11am and 2pm Tuesday through Saturday. The short **Capers Creek Nature Trail** behind Darrah Hall twists through the woods.

The **Brick Baptist Church** across from the Penn Center was built by enslaved workers in 1855 for plantation owners. Their fingerprints can still be seen on the walls. The church was later turned over to the formerly enslaved. It's home to an active congregation and not open to the public, but you can ask about popping in while exploring the Penn Center campus.

FAMOUS LOCALS

Notable figures with connections to Beaufort include Harriet Tubman, conductor of the Underground Railroad, who worked here to liberate enslaved people and recruit them into the army. Some tours may pass the home of formerly enslaved Robert Smalls, who commandeered a Confederate ship, turned it over to the Union and became the period's most inspiring African American politician.

Daufuskie Island by Golf Cart

Bouncing around Daufuskie Island in a golf cart might be the most fun you'll have in the Lowcountry. This idyllic island is a sublime day trip and a window into the Lowcountry's slower-paced past. Attractions include a historical trail, a few restaurants, a couple of golf clubs, a winery and a rum distillery. Its shores are only accessible by boat.

START	END	LENGTH
Freeport Marina	Freeport Marina	11½ miles; 4 to 5 hours

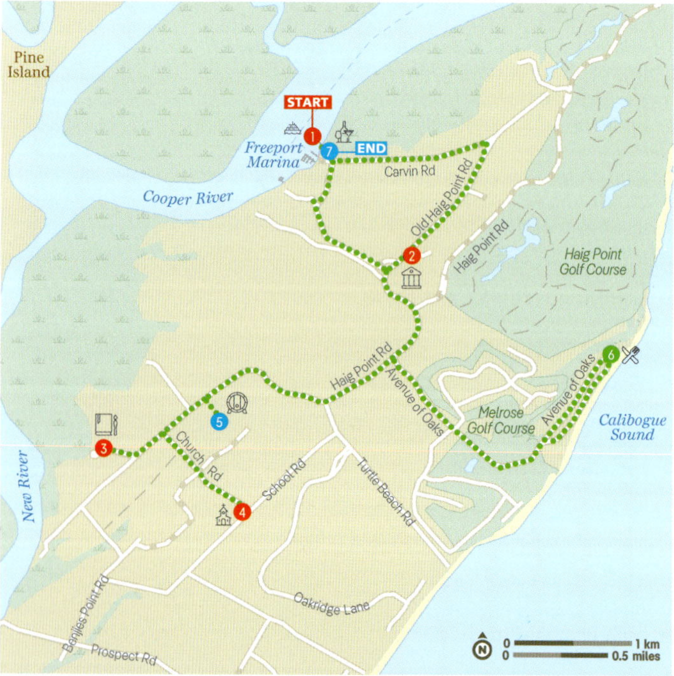

1 Freeport Marina

Water taxis from Hilton Head and Bluffton stop at this tiny marina. Most reservations include a golf cart rental option. **H2O Sports** *(h2osports.com; ferry adult/child $45/35; half-day golf cart rental $80)* gets you there in 20 minutes from Harbour Town Marina. After disembarking, you'll be handed a basic map and sent on your way. Bounce south on Carvin Rd, then turn right onto Old Haig Point Rd/ Haig Point Rd.

2 Daufuskie Island History Museum

This museum inside **Mt Carmel Baptist Church No 2** shares information about the island's prior inhabitants. Pick up a more detailed island map here, with summaries of 20 historic destinations. Continue to the historic district.

3 Sarah Grant Home

Pause by the former **residence** of Sarah Grant, who was a busy midwife and caretaker on the island in the 1900s. As locals explained, 'Granny bring em 'n she take 'em away.' The nearby segregated Daufuskie School enrolled white students from 1913 to 1962. Backtrack on Haig Point Rd to Church Rd.

4 Baptist Church & Mary Field School

Completed in 1884, the First Union African Baptist Church still holds Sunday services. The nearby **Mary Field School** educated the island's Black children from the 1930s until 1962. Author Pat Conroy (p108) began his teaching career here after integration. He shared his experiences in his book *The Water Is Wide*. Backtrack, then continue east on Haig Point Rd.

5 Daufuskie Island Distillery

Sample small-batch spirits at this pond-side **distillery** *(daufuskie rum.com; 11am-5pm Tue-Sat)*. Cocktails and tasty food-truck fare are sold here too.

6 Melrose Oyster House

From Hague Point Rd, follow the Ave of the Oaks through the former Melrose Plantation, one of 11 plantations that dotted the island. It was later converted into a resort, which was eventually abandoned. A new seafood restaurant, **Melrose Oyster House** *(melrose oysterhouse.com; 11am-3pm & 6-8pm)*, has opened near the waterfront here.

7 Old Daufuskie Crab Co

Back at the marina, this convivial **place** *(daufuskiedifference.com; 11am-8:30pm)* thrums with good cheer – possibly fueled by its potent 'Scrap Iron' punch. In the afternoon, order a drink at the outdoor bar and kick back to live music. Freeport Marina is next door. Tip: do not drink a Scrap Iron at the start of your golf-cart ride.

EXPERIENCES

Take a Pat Conroy Tour in Beaufort

TOUR

Until his death in 2016, South Carolina's literary great Pat Conroy called Beaufort home. The city inspired some of his most famous works, including *The Great Santini* and *The Prince of Tides*. On a 90-minute golf-cart excursion with **Pat Conroy's Beaufort Tour** (*beauforttoursllc.com; adult/child $40/20*), you'll motor past sites that were important in the writing life of the beloved author. Stops include his high school (where he later taught), homes in the Point neighborhood where he lived and wrote, and Beaufort National Cemetery, where his parents are buried (but not together).

Guides will encourage you to visit the **Pat Conroy Literary Center** (MAP: 1 P100 **A1**; *patconroyliterarycenter.org; 1-4pm Thu-Sun*), which has exhibits on his life and work, including his writing desk and chair, and a handwritten prologue to *The Prince of Tides*. The center also hosts readings by acclaimed authors, and events including the **Pat Conroy Literary Festival** (MAP: 2 P100 **A1**) in November.

Spend a Day on the Sea Islands

ISLANDS

A cluster of marshy, rural islands near Beaufort offer an enticing amalgam of history, culture and nature.

To the east, **St Helena Island** is the heart of Gullah country (p110), where descendants of the enslaved have painstakingly preserved their language and culture. Once housing one of the nation's first schools for the formerly enslaved, the **Penn Center** (MAP: 3 P100 **G5**; *penncenter.com; 10am-4pm Tue-Sat; tours $15-20*) is the island's historic hub. It has a small **museum** that covers Gullah culture and traces the history of Penn School. You can explore St Helena's Gullah heritage with **Gullah-N-Geechie Mahn Tours** (MAP: 4 P100 **H6**; *gullahngeechietours.com; 2hr tour $49*).

Further east, on **Hunting Island** (MAP: 5 P100 **H1**), you'll discover one of the state's most breathtaking coastal parks. To the south, **Parris Island** features a Marine Corps training ground and **museum** (MAP: 6 P100 **F2**; *mcrdpi.marines.mil/Visitors/Parris-Island-Museum/*. Check the website for entry requirements. Have

MARTIN LUTHER KING ON ST HELENA ISLAND

Martin Luther King and other freedom fighters strategized at the Penn Center numerous times during the Civil Rights Movement in the 1960s. King also worked on his *'I Have a Dream'* speech here and stayed at Gantt Cottage.

identification, vehicle registration and proof of insurance with you for entry to the military base.

Savor Seafood at the Ribaut Social Club

SEAFOOD AND STEAK

MAP: 7 P100 **C2**

Toast the good life with a cocktail on the 4th-floor terrace before dinner at the **Ribaut Social Club** *(anchorage1770.com)*. This lofty perch overlooks Port Royal Sound. The refined yet homey main dining room is tucked within a refurbished mansion and inn, **Anchorage 1770**, that once belonged to Rear Admiral Lester Beardslee (and is named after his boisterous gentleman's club). Executive chef Daniel Salazar brings a personal touch to regional, seasonal dishes.

Camp by the Beach at Hunting Island State Park

CAMP SITE

MAP: 8 P100 **H1**

You can pitch your tent beside palm trees just steps from the Atlantic at this pretty **state park campground** *(southcarolinaparks.com; rustic tent sites $50-65, campsites $80-85)*. Welcoming staff and well-maintained bathrooms are additional highlights. Other sites here are set beneath pines and further from the beach but are still within walking distance. On hot days the beach-adjacent area typically enjoys sea breezes, while the RV sites have shade. All are available by walk-up, but reservations are advisable in summer. Pack bug spray to ward off mosquitos and possibly sand fleas.

DRINKING & NIGHTLIFE

Independent nightlife on Hilton Head Island is concentrated at the southern end in an area known as the 'Barmuda Triangle', where several restaurants cluster in Hilton Head Plaza. Just east, the **Jazz Corner** (MAP: 9 P100 **E5**; *thejazzcorner.com*) is a great spot for live music and a martini. Otherwise, enjoy waterfront drinks at places like **Quarterdeck** (p111), **Coast** and **Skull Creek**.

Delve into History & Nature in Hilton Head

MUSEUM

MAP: 10 P100 **E5**

You can explore both inside and outside at the free **Coastal Discovery Museum** *(coastaldiscovery.org)*, a Smithsonian Affiliate with exhibits showcasing Hilton Head Island's rich Gullah history, natural wonders and other coastal treasures. Exhibits in the Discovery House spotlight Native American history as well as impacts from the Revolutionary and Civil Wars and details of the Reconstruction Era. A 2-mile trail on the 68-acre property winds past ancient oak trees, lush gardens and historic buildings, and you can stroll over the salt marsh on boardwalks.

Plans are afoot to share exhibits from the Santa Elena History Center in Beaufort, which were transferred here after the center closed in 2020. The exhibits will relate the little-told story of the earliest Europeans to settle in North America. In 1562 the French landed on present-day Parris Island and dubbed it Charlesfort. They abandoned the site, but in 1566 the Spanish moved in and renamed it Santa Elena.

Climb Harbour Town Lighthouse

LIGHTHOUSE

MAP: 11 P100 D6

You'll learn local history while climbing 114 steps inside Hilton Head's **lighthouse** *(harbortown lighthouse.com; $7)*. Built in 1970, this red-and-white-striped beacon is perched beside the Harbour Town marina at the island's southern end, tucked away on Sea Pines Plantation. The stairwell to the top doubles as a museum, and it is filled with Civil War artifacts, island history and regional lighthouse history. The lighthouse owes much of its modern success to Nadia Wagner, one of the country's few female lighthouse keepers. It added a Fresnel lens in 2022.

In addition to the admission fee, you'll pay a $9 day-pass fee for entry to Sea Pines. The lighthouse is open from 10am to sunset.

Crank up the Yacht Rock on a Boat Cruise

NATURE TOUR

MAP: 13 P100 F5

At Hilton Head there are scads of boat tours and charters that will get you out onto Calibogue Sound for wildlife watching, beachcombing and relaxing in the sun. How to pick a cruise? Walk down to the closest marina or yacht basin and see which outfitters are docked there.

You can relax on a beanbag chair while nodding your head to yacht rock on a half-day trip with **Native Son Adventures** *(nativeson adventures.com; trips from $350)*. On the well-run 'Day with a Native' tour you can choose your own adventure. You can cruise to Shell Island, which is fantastic for beachcombing, and to Vanishing Island, a pretty but ephemeral sandbar. You can also relax on Daufuskie Island or hunt for shark teeth. Guides point out dolphins as you motor across the sound. They'll also pack a stand-up paddleboard if you're interested. Trips leave from Shelter Cove Marina. Alcohol is BYOB.

GULLAH CULTURE

Starting in the 16th century, African people were forcibly transported from the region known as the Rice Coast (Sierra Leone, Senegal, Gambia and Angola) to a landscape of remote islands. These new African Americans retained many of their homeland traditions after the fall of slavery. The resulting culture of Gullah (known as Geechee in Georgia) has its own language – an English-based Creole with many African words and sentence structures – and many traditions. Beaufort's **Original Gullah Festival** (MAP: 12 P100 C2) in May celebrates Gullah culture.

Best Places for...

$ Budget $$ Midrange $$$ Top End

Eating

Beaufort

Lowcountry Produce $
14 D2
A fantastic cafe and market for picnics with an equally appealing cafe. Indulge in an Oooey Gooey, a grilled pimento-cheese sandwich with bacon and garlic-pepper jelly. *11am-2:30pm*

Blacksheep x Sabbatical $
15 F1
This small wine shop and restaurant serves a deliciously eclectic selection of toasts, sips and sandwiches downtown. *11am-6pm Tue-Sat*

Old Bull Tavern $$
16 C2
Delicious food and cocktails with a wood-fired pizza oven and low-lit, worldly aesthetic. Menu changes daily but always features playful American and European comfort dishes. *5-9pm Tue-Sat*

Hilton Head

Fat Baby's Pizza & Subs $
17 E6
In the center of the island, pick up big to-go sandwiches for your boat excursion. *11am-9pm Mon-Sat*

Hudson's $$

Hilton Head's go-to seafood shack, with a wonderful dockside deck on the water that brims with revelry. And loads of just-off-the-boat seafood. *11am-9pm Mon-Sat, 10-9pm Sun*

Skull Creek $$
see 18 E4
In a renovated old river house, this restaurant serves mouthwatering American, Italian and Southern dishes. *11am-9pm Mon-Sat, 10am-9pm Sun*

Coast $$
19 E6
Listen to live music while savoring elevated seafood and Lowcountry dishes on a sparkling patio by the sea. In the Sea Pines Resort. *11:30am-4pm & 4-9pm*

Drinking

Beaufort

Hemingway's
20 C3
Beaufort's best little dive fills nightly with local characters. *11am-2am*

Hilton Head

Harbour Town Bakery & Cafe
see 11 D6
Grab a specialty coffee and a pastry at this cute cottage in the Sea Pines Resort. *7am-2:30pm*

Quarterdeck
see 11 D6
Fresh from a glossy makeover, this Sea Pines spot is the place to see, be seen and enjoy a post-beach cocktail. *11:30am-10pm*

Salty Dog Cafe

Sip cocktails and beer on the patio beside South Beach Marina at this hopping spot at Braddock's Cove. Service can be brisk. *8am-9pm*

Explore Savannah

Savannah's Walking Tour

Wormsloe State Historic Site (p150)
SERGE SKIBA/SHUTTERSTOCK ©

See p130 for eating, drinking and shopping listings

Explore Historic & Power Plant Districts

Fringed by Forsyth Park to the south, Savannah's Historic District is home to 22 gorgeous squares flanked by exquisite 18th- and 19th-century homes, fascinating museums and monuments, and world-class restaurants, all enveloped by a canopy of Spanish-moss-laden live oak trees. It's the Southern Gothic heart of the city. Overlooking the Savannah River, the new Power Plant District elbowed its way onto the scene in 2021. This showy entertainment hub revitalized a quarter-mile strip of riverfront, and there isn't a live oak in sight. The JW Marriott Hotel is the district's anchor and its lobby a dazzling showpiece.

Getting Around

Walking

The best way to explore is on foot, which gives you an up-close look at historic squares and grand homes. Sidewalks are plentiful. A paved walkway fronts the Savannah River.

Bus

The JMR Transit Center just west of the Historic District is the city's local transport hub. You can catch the free 'DOT' line for rides all around the area and to Forsyth Park.

Taxis, Pedicabs & Bikes

These are other convenient ways to get around if you're staying nearby.

THE BEST

PARK Forsyth Park (p118)

UNEXPECTED SIGHTS Plant Riverside Disrict (p121)

MUSEUM Telfair Academy (p126)

RESTAURANT Grey (p128)

BAR Alley Cat Lounge (p131)

Forsyth Park (p118)

Plant Riverside District
Savannah Smiles Dueling Pianos
13
31
Savannah River
Riverwalk
W River St
W Bay St
Williamson St
Indian St
W Bryan St
American Prohibition Museum
4
Franklin Sq
City Market
Ellis Sq
W St Julian St
W Congress St
W Congress La
Orange St
Zubley St
The Grey
10
Martin Luther King Jr Blvd
W Broughton St
Jefferson St
19
25
Barnard St
29
Whitaker St
Bull St
Johnson Sq
E River St
E Bay St
Emmet Park
14
26
17
E St Julian St
Reynolds Sq
E Bryan St
E Congress St
23
E Congress La
22
E Broughton St
Lincoln St
E Broughton La
Oglethorpe Sq
E State St
Columbia Sq
E York St
E York La
E Oglethorpe Ave
Juliette Gordon Low Birthplace Museum
7
16
20
Wright Sq
W York St
33
W Broughton La
28
Telfair Academy
2
Telfair Sq
W State St
Montgomery St
Jepson Center for the Arts
3
Savannah Civic Center
Orleans Sq
W Oglethorpe La
Hull St
Chippewa Sq
Greyhound Bus Station
W Oglethorpe Ave
12
Fahm St
Ann St
Pappy St
W Turner Blvd
Turner Blvd
SCAD Museum of Art
9
Amtrak (3mi)
Savannah Visitors Center
Louisville Rd
0 200 m
0 0.1 miles
A B C D E F
1 2 3 4

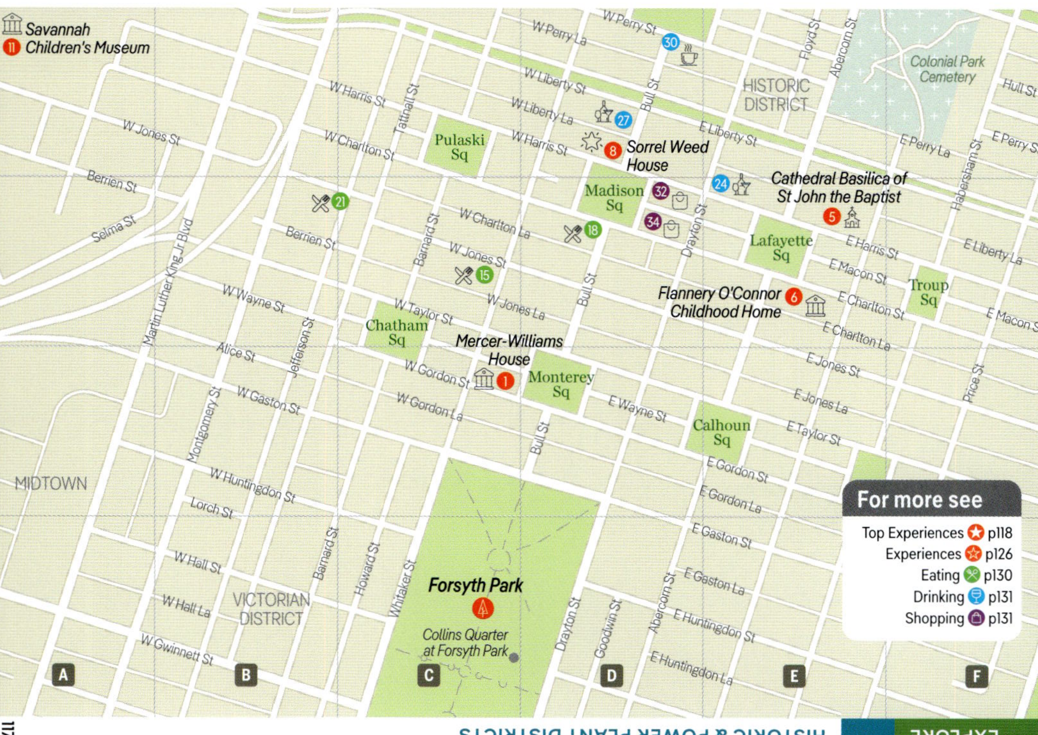
Savannah Children's Museum
HISTORIC DISTRICT
Colonial Park Cemetery
Sorrel Weed House
Cathedral Basilica of St John the Baptist
Flannery O'Connor Childhood Home
Mercer-Williams House
Forsyth Park
Collins Quarter at Forsyth Park
MIDTOWN
VICTORIAN DISTRICT
Pulaski Sq
Madison Sq
Lafayette Sq
Troup Sq
Chatham Sq
Monterey Sq
Calhoun Sq
W Perry St
W Perry La
W Liberty St
W Liberty La
W Harris St
W Charlton St
W Charlton La
W Jones St
W Jones La
W Taylor St
W Wayne St
W Gordon St
W Gordon La
W Gaston St
W Huntingdon St
W Hall St
W Hall La
W Gwinnett St
Berrien St
Selma St
Alice St
Lorch St
Martin Luther King Jr Blvd
Montgomery St
Jefferson St
Tattnall St
Barnard St
Howard St
Whitaker St
Bull St
Drayton St
Goodwin St
Abercorn St
Floyd St
Habersham St
Price St
Hull St
E Perry St
E Perry La
E Liberty St
E Liberty La
E Harris St
E Macon St
E Charlton St
E Charlton La
E Jones St
E Jones La
E Wayne St
E Taylor St
E Gordon St
E Gordon La
E Gaston St
E Gaston La
E Huntingdon St
E Huntingdon La
For more see
Top Experiences p118
Experiences p126
Eating p130
Drinking p131
Shopping p131

★ TOP EXPERIENCE

Forsyth Park

Lush and inviting, Forsyth Park buzzes with activity year-round. The sprawling green lawns, historic monuments and majestic fountain are the heart and soul of downtown Savannah's outdoor life. Come here for recreation, to bask in the sun or simply to stroll around the paths and soak up the splendor.

MAP P116 **C8**

PLANNING TIP
Forsyth Park is at the southern edge of the Historic District between Drayton and Whitaker Sts. Pick a patch of grass on the north side near the fountain for some shade and a more intimate feel.

Scan this QR code for further information.

Inspired Design

Developed in the 1840s on 10 acres of land donated to the city by Savannah scholar-diplomat William Hodgson, Forsyth Park was part of Oglethorpe's original vision for the city and was expanded after Georgia governor John Forsyth donated an additional 20 acres that tripled the size of the park. In conceiving Forsyth's layout, Bavarian landscape designer William Bischoff took cues from the French. He was inspired by urban-renewal efforts taking place in Paris that featured neighborhoods radiating out from a central green space.

In 1858 a fountain was installed, and over the years monuments to commemorate historic events in Savannah have been added.

The Famous Fountain

Forsyth's central fountain is the park's crown jewel and has become a distinctive icon of Savannah – but it's not quite as unique as people think.

When the fountain was decided upon in 1858, the city council appointed a committee to choose a design...from a catalog. The design, simply known as 'No 5,' was one of a few elaborate options featured in a catalog of ornamental ironwork by Janes,

DENNIS MACDONALD/SHUTTERSTOCK ©

Beebe & Company of New York. Modeled after a fountain designed by Michel Joseph Napoléon Liénard and cast by the JPV André Iron Foundry in Paris, its inspiration was sourced during the Great Exhibition of 1851 at Crystal Palace in London after a Janes, Beebe & Company representative was sent to research the manufacturing of garden ornaments.

Playtime, a Splash Pad & Gardens

Large grassy areas blanket the park, and they're ready-made for picnics, frisbee throwing and letting the kids run wild. You'll also find tennis courts and basketball courts. There are **two playgrounds**, located south of the fountain. One is accessible for all children, including those in wheelchairs – kids can let loose on its slides, swings and climbers. A **splash pad** beside the

QUICK BREAK

Pick up a terrific brew inside **Sentient Bean** *(sentientbean.com; 7am-7pm)*. With its spacious boho interior, trendy clientele and baristas and nods to sustainability, it's a perfect indie coffeehouse. It's across from the park on E Park Ave.

STAYING SAFE
You can enjoy the park by day or in the evening, but it's best not to linger past midnight.

GREENING OF THE FOUNTAIN
Since the 1980s the Savannah St Patrick's Day Committee has dyed the waters of the Forsyth Fountain emerald green every year to celebrate the start of St Patrick's season in March.

amphitheater bandshell on the eastern side of the park keeps kids cool during hot summers. There are **restrooms** near the splash pad, beside Collins Quarter at Forsyth.

The **Garden of Fragrance** was created with blind visitors in mind, but all can enjoy the varied floral scents of the plants here. Scents are protected within the garden's three walls. A wrought-iron ornamental gate marks the entrance. The garden is open from 9am to 2pm Monday through Friday.

Saturday Farmers Market

You'll likely hear a friendly 'How ya doin'?' while strolling between vendor booths at the Forsyth Farmers Market, where local producers sell tomatoes, okra, watermelons, eggs and more from 9am to 1pm year-round. You'll find their booths lining the central sidewalk at the southern end of the park, between the Civil War Memorial to the Confederate Dead and E Park Ave.

Grab Coffee & a Bite

Tucked inside the park, the new **Collins Quarter at Forsyth Park** *(thecollinsquarter.com; brunch 9am-3pm Tue-Thu, 8am-3pm Fri-Mon)* serves crab cakes Benedict, chicken and waffles and other decadent Southern dishes – plus cocktails – at its daily brunch. This is patio dining at its finest.

★ TOP EXPERIENCE

Plant Riverside District

An entertainment hub centered on a dazzling JW Marriott and a trio of buildings along River St dubbed the Three Muses, the new Plant Riverside District is generating some serious buzz. To find the property at night, just look for the illuminated smokestacks.

MAP P116 **C1**

JW Marriott Lobby Exhibits

Stepping into the generator hall at this former power plant is a big 'Whoa!,' especially if you're walking in from the riverfront or the leafy Historic District. Throngs of people flow past as they explore the vast space, and there's an enormous chrome-dipped dinosaur hanging overhead. Glittering geodes and minerals beckon in every direction. Doubling as a public exhibit hall, this grand space is also the lobby of the **JW Marriott Plant Riverside**, which opened in 2021.

The **dinosaur** hanging overhead is a replica of a 135 ft-tall *Amphicoelias fragillimus*, the largest species of dinosaur ever discovered, and each of its 230 bones have been dipped in chrome. This fancy beast did not roam the Georgia coast, but hotelier and Plant Riverside developer Richard Kressler, a Savannah native, is a collector of fossils and minerals. Specimens from his vast collection, some dating back millions of years, are on display across the lobby like exhibits in a very hip natural history museum.

The scene is touristy, and it's not 100% beloved by locals, but the over-the-top exuberance can be kind of fun. The lobby is definitely worth a look.

PLANNING TIP
Drivers will find nearly 500 spaces at the **Plant Riverside Parking Garage** *(3hr/6hr/overnight $10/20/45)* just northwest of the JW Marriott. Credit cards only.

OSTROWS2/SHUTTERSTOCK ©

Shops & Galleries

Galleries, boutiques and exuberant works of art fill the cavernous lobby, which exudes steam-punk cool with its mix of modern amenities and original power plant fixtures. One eye-catching holdover is the power plant's original switch-board. Many glittery showpieces are displayed in compact galleries that resemble transparent jewel boxes.

Several shops within the hotel complex – which includes three buildings known collectively as the Three Muses – are local to Savannah or support Savannah artists. If you're hungry, swing by the Plant Riverside outpost of **Byrd Cookies** *(byrdcookiecompany.com)*, a Savannah company that celebrated its centennial in 2024. Byrd sells an array of small, round cookies, and their shops are known for their free samples. Savannah artist Amelia Jamerson – she was born and raised in Savannah and graduated from the Savannah College of Art & Design (SCAD) – sells her whimsical creations, including prints, cards and stickers, in a little shop of love and happiness on the riverfront at **18Loves Art** *(18loves.com)*.

Rooftop Bars

Pastel pillows and plush cabanas infuse the **Myrtle & Rose Rooftop Bar** *(plantriverside.com/restaurant-bar/electric-moon/)* with an inviting, breezy ambience. The graceful Talmadge Bridge spans the river just north of the bar, and cargo ships and paddleboats ply the waterway below. This chic spot serves a champagne brunch on weekends. The bar sits on the roof of the Three Muses complex. The nearby **Electric Moon Skytop Lounge** *(plantriverside.com/music-entertainment/#dlevents)*, perched on the roof of the JW Marriott, is sexy yet whimsical – it's a thing – with its slide, spiral staircase and canary-yellow lounges.

Live Music & Shows

On an evening stroll along the river you'll likely hear musicians strumming their guitars at watering holes that overlook the busy waterway. The indoor music venue here, **District Live Powered by Live Nation** (pictured; *plantriverside.com/music-entertainment/*), hosts touring acts with regional and national followings.

Splash Pad

If you're staying downtown with kids, and they're getting fussy from the heat, lead the gang to the free splash pad. You'll find it on the River Walk side of the Power Plant District, in front of the Three Muses buildings.

QUICK BREAK
The oom-pah-pah Bavarian theme may not match the vibe of Savannah's historic areas, but Oktoberfest music and a giant pretzel do set a festive mood at **Riverside Biergarten** *(plantriverside.com/restaurant-bar/riverside-biergarten)*, which offers fine views of the Savannah River and passing crowds.

Walk Savannah's Squares

One of the joys of visiting Savannah is walking around the historic district amid some of the most beautiful residential architecture in the country. The city's original layout is an inspiring bit of urban planning: four open squares, each ensconced within four residential and four civic blocks. It's a pattern that has repeated itself as Savannah has grown.

START	END	LENGTH
Forsyth Park	Johnson Sq	1¾ miles; 2 hours

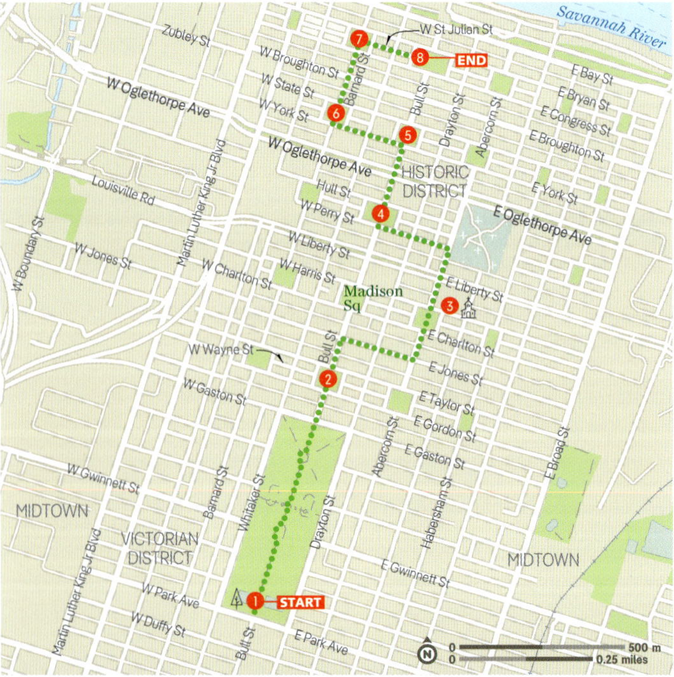

1 Forsyth Park

Begin this leisurely stroll at the southern entrance to **Forsyth Park** at Bull St and Park Ave. Walk north along the main pathway and arrive at the iconic fountain.

2 Monterey Square

Continue north on Bull St toward the intersection with Wayne St, where a monument topped by a statue of General Casimir Pulaski soars above the square. The **Mercer-Williams House**, setting of the novel and film *Midnight in the Garden of Good and Evil*, faces the west side.

3 Cathedral Basilica of St John the Baptist

Walk north and turn right on cobblestoned Jones St, which is flanked by Greek Revival homes and live oaks. Turn left on Abercorn to see the twin steeples of the spectacular **Cathedral Basilica of St John the Baptist**. Head north to Colonial Park Cemetery at the intersection of Perry St. Wander past Gothic tombs and monuments, then turn west on E Perry St.

4 Chippewa Square

A bronze statue of Savannah founder James Oglethorpe oversees all the action from **Chippewa Square**, which sits in the middle of the Historic District. This park is famous for the park-bench scenes in the 1994 film *Forest Gump*, shot on the north side along Hull St, but the actual bench was a prop and is no longer in the park.

5 Wright Square

Keep truckin' north on Bull St past Oglethorpe Ave to York St and arrive at **Wright Square**. This was the second square constructed in the city and is the burial site of Tomochichi, the Yamacraw tribe leader who befriended Oglethorpe and helped him establish the colony.

6 Telfair Square

Head west on York St for two blocks to **Telfair Square**. You won't find any monuments with a contentious backstory here, but there is creative inspiration all around – both the **Telfair Academy** and the **Jepson Center for the Arts** border Barnard St.

7 Ellis Square

Continue north on Barnard St and cross Broughton St, downtown's main commercial drag, toward Congress St to arrive at **Ellis Square**. It was a center of commerce from the 1730s through the 1950s. In the 1850s it housed a market for the sale of enslaved human beings.

8 Johnson Square

Head back east down St Julian St toward Bull St and end at **Johnson Square**, Savannah's first and largest square.

EXPERIENCES

Tour the Mercer-Wiliams House

HISTORIC HOME

MAP: 1 P116 **C7**

You're stepping into a former crime scene at the **Mercer-Williams House** *(mercerhouse.com; $13.50)*, the one-time home of Jim Williams, the Savannah art dealer portrayed by Kevin Spacey in the film version of *Midnight in the Garden of Good and Evil*. Williams died back in 1990, but his infamous mansion didn't become a museum until 2004. The success of the book, which was on the *New York Times* bestseller list for 216 weeks, launched Savannah's ongoing run as a travel darling. You cannot visit the upstairs, where Williams' family still lives, but the downstairs is an interior decorator's fantasy. Tours are a brisk 35 minutes. Enter from the carriage house behind the home.

Find the Bird Girl at the Telfair Academy

MUSEUM

MAP: 2 P116 **D3**

It's easy to miss the famous but low-key Bird Girl statue on your first loop around the Sculpture Gallery at the **Telfair Academy** *(telfair.org; adult/child $30/10; 10am-5pm Wed-Mon)*, considered Savannah's top art museum. But be sure to find her – there's something captivating about her simple visage. She drew hordes of admirers to Bonaventure Cemetery (p146), her first home, but after she was selected to adorn the cover of *Midnight in the Garden of Good & Evil*, the decision was made to move the statue and protect her here.

Ensconced in the historic Telfair family mansion, the museum is filled with 19th-century American art and silver and a smattering of European pieces. The home itself is gorgeous and sunrise-hued – an artifact in its own right that wows visitors to this day. You'll want to sit for a minute to soak up the grandeur of the large canvases and setting in the soaring Rotunda Gallery.

Admission to the museum includes unlimited entries to the Jepson Center (p126) and the Owens-Thomas House for a week.

Immerse Yourself in Contemporary Art at the Jepson Center

GALLERY

MAP: 3 P116 **D3**

Luminous green lily pads and red-orange tulips seem within your grasp in the delightful Landscape Gallery at the **Jepson Center** *(JCA; telfair.org; adult/child $30/10)*. Within the Jepson's new Children's Art Museum (CAM), it's an immersive introduction to Impressionism geared to kids and anyone who appreciates art. And the Jepson overall? Designed by the great Moshe Safdie, and looking pretty darn space-age by Savannah's standards, the JCA focuses on 20th- and 21st-century art. Be on the lookout for wandering SCAD design students and temporary exhibitions covering topics from race to art in various media.

At lunchtime you can nibble at a vegetable grain bowl or a chicken-salad sandwich in the bright and airy **Wildflower Cafe** *(wildflowercafesavannah.com)* beside the entrance. It's open Wednesday through Sunday. Your ticket allows entry to the Telfair Academy and the Owens-Thomas House for one week.

Sip a Bees Knees in the American Prohibition Museum

MUSEUM

MAP: 4 P116 **D2**

If you walk around the City Market you'll likely pass a couple of folks dressed in Prohibition-era duds standing outside this **museum** *(americanprohibitionmuseum.com; adult $18, with cocktail $30, child $11)* and touting its wonders – and it all looks a little hokey at first glance. But then they mention that your admission can include a cocktail in a recreated speakeasy and the whole shebang suddenly seems more fun. But even without the drink this museum delivers. You'll learn the history of Prohibition in the US, and it's fascinating. Exhibits are engaging for the most part, from the historic black-and-white video clips to the detailed wax figures that look as though they're up to mischief. You'll step into a speakeasy, named Up, at the end of your visit for your bartender-crafted cocktail.

Admire the Cathedral Basilica of St John the Baptist

CHURCH

MAP: 5 P116 **E6**

Even if you're rushing around downtown, the architectural beauty of this French Gothic **cathedral** *(savannahcathedral.org; 9-11:30am & 1-4:30pm Mon-Sat, 1-4:30pm Sun)* and its twin spires will likely trigger a nod of appreciation, if not a full stop and a 'Wow!' Inside there are wonders in every direction. Highlights include the stunning stained-glass transept windows from Austria depicting Christ's ascension into heaven and the ornate Stations of the Cross woodcarvings from Bavaria. The cathedral was completed in 1896 but destroyed by fire two years later. It reopened in 1912.

HISTORIC DISTRICT TOURS

Learn about the side of Savannah that didn't make the history books with Vaughnette Goode-Walker's **Footprints of Savannah** *(footprintsofsavannah.com; adult/child $30/10)*, a 1½-hour walking tour that highlights the city's rich and complex African American history. If you prefer to learn on wheels, **Savannah Bike Tours** *(savannahbiketours.com; adult/child $45/25)* offers two-hour cycling excursions over easy, flat terrain in its fleet of cruisers.

NOTEWORTHY HOUSE TOURS

Flannery O'Connor Childhood Home

MAP: 6 P116 E6

This stone row house on Lafayette Sq is where the literary great was born in 1925 and lived until she was 13.

Juliette Gordon Low Birthplace Museum

MAP: 7 P116 E4

Childhood home of the founder of the Girl Scouts of the USA, which runs the museum.

Sorrel Weed House

MAP: 8 P116 D5

Fans of the paranormal can get their thrills at one of Savannah's spookiest mansions.

The illuminated exterior is quite impressive at night.

You can admire the cathedral's treasures on a self-guided tour during opening hours. Docent-led tours can be arranged. A $3 donation is appreciated if you visit.

Dig into Dark History TOUR

Sketchy parking lots, weathered cemeteries and eerie town squares: it's just another day at the office for Brandon Carter, owner and lead guide at **Savannah True History Tours** *(savannahtruehistory.com; adult/child $28/free)*, which offers a two-hour Dark History tour that dives into the facts behind the city's most gruesome stories. You'll hear about a serial killer, Sherman's occupation of the city during the Civil War and a controversial exhumation in Monterey Sq – and that's just a sampling.

Ghost tours swarm the Historic District at night, many of them quite theatrical, and Carter has some fun poking holes – 'That's not true!' – in the outlandish tales you'll overhear as you pound the pavement. A local attorney and former National Park Service ranger, Carter also leads history tours, pub tours and cemetery tours.

See What's New at the SCAD Museum of Art MUSEUM

MAP: 9 P116 B4

Step inside this architecturally striking (what else would you expect from this school of design?) **museum** *(scadmoa.org; adult/child $10/free;10am-5pm)* for your contemporary art fix. This brick, steel, concrete and glass longhouse provides creative sitting areas inside and out, and a number of rotating and visiting exhibitions that showcase some of the most impressive talents within the contemporary-art world.

Dine at The Grey MODERN AMERICAN

MAP: 10 P116 C2

Staff members make you feel instantly at home inside **The Grey** *(thegreyrestaurant.com)*, and this wonderfully retro makeover of the city's 1930s Greyhound Bus Terminal is one of Savannah's culinary darlings. Here, chef Mashama Bailey's 'Port City Southern' cuisine is a delightful, immigrant-infused take on local grub. Dapper bartenders work the best seats in the house, around the U-shaped centerpiece bar, where scrumptious lamb shoulder and a gargantuan pork shank are standouts. Reservations essential.

If you don't have reservations, you can try to nab a seat at The Grey's first-come first-served **Diner Bar**, which overlooks Martin Luther King Jr Blvd. It has a short menu of snacks and entrées.

Devour Donuts at The Thunderbird Inn HOTEL

MAP: 12 P116 **A3**

Go ahead, take that saucy donut, the one slathered in chocolate and sprinkles. You know you want it. Yep, donuts topped with decadent frosting are what's for breakfast at **The Thunderbird Inn** *(thethunderbirdinn.com)*. 'A tad Palm Springs, a touch Vegas' best describes this vintage-chic 1964 motel that wins its own popularity contest – a 'Hippest hotel in Savannah' proclamation greets guests in the '60s-soundtracked lobby. Moon Pies and RC Colas await in every room.

In a land of stuffy B&Bs and sleek boutique hotels, this groovy place is an oasis, made all the better by local SCAD student art. If you've got an indie traveler's heart and you don't need glossy trappings, give this motel a whirl.

BEST FOR CHILDREN

Savannah Children's Museum

MAP: 11 P116 **A5**

Mostly outdoor museum in Tricentennial Park with interactive activities geared to younger children *(facebook.com/SavannahChildrensMuseum; $7.50)*.

Forsyth Park

MAP: P116 **C8**

The sprawling green space in Savannah's 'Central Park' is great for picnics and running around. There's a playground too.

Jepson Center for the Arts

see 3 **D3**

At the center's Children's Art Museum, cool immersive paintings encourage creativity. Kid 'drop-in' studios are open on weekends, and there's an art-themed story time on Fridays at 10:30am *(telfair.org; adult/child/under 6 $30/10/free)*.

Party with Savannah Smiles Dueling Pianos BAR

MAP: 13 P116 **D1**

You'll join the fun at this **dueling piano bar** *(savannahsmilesduelingpianos.com)*, where patrons decide what's played on the stage. This show brings the party crowd from far and wide. The lively space can host up to 450 people and it's a ruckus when everyone's that special kind of 'turnt,' crammed cheek by jowl and singing up a storm.

See p116 for map of locations

Best Places for...

$ Budget $$ Midrange $$$ Top End

Eating

Southern US

Treylor Park $
14 F2
Amid a retro-chic, Airstream aesthetic, enjoy Southern classics done well: fried chicken on a biscuit with sausage gravy and spicy collard greens. Pair with an excellent cocktail in the courtyard. *11am-1am Mon-Fri, 10am-1am Sat & Sun*

Mrs Wilkes Dining Room $$
15 C6
Once the lunch bell rings and you're seated family-style, the kitchen unloads fried chicken, beef stew, meatloaf, cheese potatoes, collard greens, black-eyed peas, biscuits and more. *11am-2pm Mon-Fri*

Husk Savannah $$$

16 D4
Hyperlocal, agriculturally driven Southern food sorcery with a raw seafood bar in a historic, three-story space. *5-10pm daily plus 10am-2pm Sat & Sun*

Olde Pink House $$$
17 F3
Classic Southern food done upscale in one of Savannah's most consistently great restaurants. Dine in the slender digs upstairs or go underground to the tavern. *11am-2:30pm & 5-10:30pm Tue-Sat, to 11pm Fri & Sat*

Cafes

Gryphon $
18 D6
Staffed by SCAD students, Gryphon serves gourmet salads and sandwiches, and Southern entrées like Gulf shrimp in Gouda grits. The chicken salad is always a good choice. *11am-6pm Mon-Sat, 10am-3pm Sun*

Dottie's Market $
19 D3
Kamala Harris enjoyed the salted-chocolate-caramel cake at this all-day cafe named for the owner's grandmother. Menu includes hot chicken biscuits and crab-rice salad. *8am-3pm Wed-Mon*

Collins Quarter $$
20 D4
Australian owned, this cafe turns Brooklyn coffee into beloved flat whites and long blacks. Also serves excellent fusion fare, including a drool-inducing brisket burger. Cocktails too. *9am-3pm Tue-Thu, 8am-3pm Fri-Mon*

Burgers

Crystal Beer Parlor $
21 C6
Ground chuck, lamb, bison and veggie – patty options are varied at this casual favorite, with city roots dating back to the early 1900s. Try the crab dip. *11am-9pm Tue-Sun*

Ice Cream

Leopold's Ice Cream $
22 F3
Classic American ice-cream parlor that's been scooping its creamy Greek recipes since 1919. Tutti frutti was invented here. The picks? Coconut, and honey and almond cream. *noon-9pm Mon-Thu, 1am-10pm Fri-Sun*

Drinking

Bar

Abe's on Lincoln

23 F3

Attracts an eclectic crowd that stares through boozy goggles at whatever weird behavior the bartenders are tolerating that night. *4pm-3am Mon-Sat*

Original Pinkie Masters

24 E6

Cheap, cash-only drinks and great people-watching make this hometown dive the best in town. *1pm-3am Mon-Thu, noon-3am Fri & Sat*

Cocktails

Alley Cat Lounge

25 D3

Walk down the alley, descend the steps and stroll into an underground lair humming with conviviality. *4pm-1am Mon-Thu, to 2am Fri & Sat*

Bar Julian

26 F2

Top-notch cocktails complement spectacular views of the Savannah River from this rooftop bar atop the Thompson Hotel at the eastern edge of the river walk. *7am-11pm Sun-Thu, to midnight Fri & Sat*

Artillery

 D5

Mixologists craft novel, quality cocktails in this opulent space where elements of 19th-century eclecticism and romanticism meld with modern design touches. *4-11pm Mon-Thu, to midnight Fri & Sat*

El-Rocko Lounge

 D3

You'll feel the '70s-inspired swank, but then realize that the vibe – in true Savannah fashion – is absolutely chill. *5pm-midnight Mon-Wed, to 3am Thu-Sat*

Coffee

Coffee Fox

 D3

Locally roasted coffee served in a corner shop on bustling Broughton Ave. Former site of Tondee's Tavern, where the Sons of Liberty gathered in the Colonial era. *7am-9pm Mon-Sat, 8am-6pm Sun*

Gallery Espresso

 D5

SCAD students, tourists, the downtown business crowd and Savannah's artistic elite all camp out in the cozy wingback chairs of this bohemian corner cafe. *7:30am-8pm Mon-Thu, to 9pm Fri-Sun*

Shopping

Books

Books on Bay

 D1

Junkies of that old-book smell will get a great fix at this quaint shop specializing in titles that date from the 17th century through the 1920s. *10am-5pm*

Shaver Booksellers

32 D6

Say hello to the resident cats – including Skimbleshanks – while exploring the warren of rooms composing this community-favorite bookstore. *10:30am-6pm Mon-Sat, noon-5pm Sun*

Gifts

Savannah Bee Company

33 D3

The flagship store for the internationally renowned honey purveyor. Expect artisanal honey of infinite variety and limitless free tastings. *10am-8pm Mon-Sat, to 6pm Sun*

ShopSCAD

 D6

All the wares are designed by students, faculty and alumni of Savannah's college of art and design. *10am-5pm Mon-Sat, noon-5pm Sun*

See p141
for eating, drinking and shopping listings

Explore Victorian & Starland Districts

The residential architecture is astounding in the Victorian District, which was Savannah's first suburb and today is abuzz with a vibrant arts community and up-and-coming businesses. Admire the majestic homes from Forsyth Park to Victory Dr, the area's grand, palm-tree-lined avenue, and explore the galleries, museums, shops and restaurants. The burgeoning Starland District, which stretches from Victory Dr to 37th St within the greater Midtown area, is a hub of creativity, from the bustling Starland Yard food-truck park to the unique shops and galleries catering to an enthusiastic, art-minded community.

Getting Around

Walking

With sidewalks fronting most blocks, it's easy to walk around the Victorian District and Starland. It's 1 mile from the riverfront to the Victorian District and 2 miles from the riverfront to Starland.

Bus

Buses 4, 11 and 14 run from downtown to points further south, passing through Starland and the surrounding Midtown area.

THE BEST

FOR CONTEMPLATION Laurel Grove Cemetery (p136)

MUSEUM Savannah African Art Museum (p138)

SPORTING EVENT Savannah Bananas game (p139)

BREWERY Two Tides Brewing Co (p140)

ECLECTIC SHOPPING Graveface Records & Curiosities (p140)

Victorian house

For more see
Top Experiences p136
Experiences p138
Eating p141
Drinking p141
Shopping p141
Laurel Grove Cemetery
Cemetery north entrance
Cemetery south entrance
Floyd "Press Boy" Adams Park
MIDTOWN
Enlargement
0 100 m
MIDTOWN
5 Sulfur Studios
18
2 Vittoria Pizzeria
1 Starland Yard
9 Graveface Records & Curiosities
4 First Friday
17
12 Starlandia Supply
10 Superbloom
Two Tides Brewing Co 8
11 Starland Strange & Bazaar
Kollock St
W 37th St
204
Ogeechee Rd
W 35th St
W 36th St
W 38th St
Lavinia St
Wearing Ct
W 32nd St
Kline St
Bulloch St
Harden St
Florance St
Burroughs St
W 37th St
W 38th St
W 39th St
W 40th St
W 41st St
W 42nd St
West Victory Dr
Martin Luther King Jr Blvd
W 46th St
Howard St
W 40th St
De Soto Ave
Bull St
E 40th St
W 40th St
Whitaker St
W 40th La
Maupas Ave
W 41st St
Maupas La
E 41st St
0 500 m
0 0.2 miles

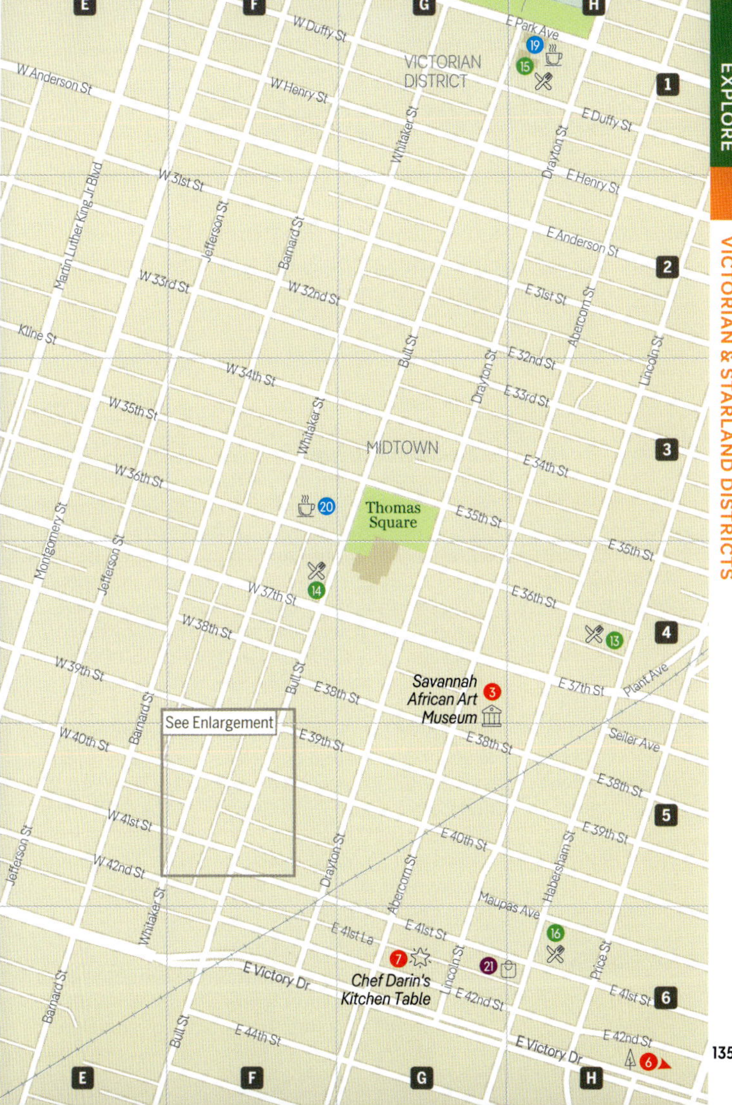
VICTORIAN DISTRICT
MIDTOWN
Thomas Square
Savannah African Art Museum
Chef Darin's Kitchen Table
See Enlargement
E Park Ave
W Duffy St
E Duffy St
W Henry St
E Henry St
W Anderson St
E Anderson St
W 31st St
E 31st St
W 32nd St
E 32nd St
W 33rd St
E 33rd St
W 34th St
E 34th St
W 35th St
E 35th St
W 36th St
E 36th St
W 37th St
E 37th St
W 38th St
E 38th St
W 39th St
E 39th St
W 40th St
E 40th St
W 41st St
E 41st St
W 42nd St
E 42nd St
E 41st La
E 44th St
E Victory Dr
Maupas Ave
Seiler Ave
Plant Ave
Kline St
Martin Luther King Jr Blvd
Montgomery St
Jefferson St
Barnard St
Whitaker St
Bull St
Drayton St
Abercorn St
Lincoln St
Habersham St
Price St

★ TOP EXPERIENCE

Laurel Grove Cemetery

While it may not have as much pop-culture hype and natural beauty as Bonaventure, Laurel Grove Cemetery is worth a visit for its spectacular monuments and rich history. Developed in 1850, it was the city's primary burial ground and many of Savannah's notable citizens were interred here.

MAP P134 **C1**

PLANNING TIP
Try to visit either section of the cemetery first thing in the morning or last thing before it closes – the light creates longer shadows for a more atmospheric effect.

Scan this QR code for further information.

A Necropolis Divided

Laurel Grove *(8am-5pm)* is divided into two sections, north and south, by a highway. But more than a road divides them: Laurel Grove North was exclusively for whites and Laurel Grove South for blacks. The cemetery has two separate entrances.

The land that forms Laurel Grove today was once the Springfield Plantation, owned by one of Savannah's early colonists. Four acres of the original cemetery (the lowest, most ill-drained point in a natural gorge, furthest from the city) was designated for the city's African American population, both free and enslaved. This was to replace the original graveyard in present-day Whitefield and Calhoun Sqs, which prevented the southward expansion of the city. The acreage was increased to 15 and then doubled a few years later. The present allotment of 90 acres is roughly the same as for Laurel Grove North.

Here Rests Savannah Society

Many notable Savannahians have been interred in both sections of Laurel Grove. On the north side the most famed is Juliette Gordon Low, founder

DNDAVIS/SHUTTERSTOCK ©

of the Girl Scouts of the USA, and more than 1500 Confederate soldiers are buried in a section devoted entirely to Civil War servicemen.

In the south cemetery are the graves of enslaved people and other African Americans who played an important role in the community's history, including Andrew Bryan, founder of the First African Baptist Church, and WW Law, a prominent leader in Savannah's Civil Rights movement. A wooden cross reading 'Stranger Burials' marks the 60-acre pauper burial grounds, which hold about 4600 unknown dead.

All the plots in Laurel Grove North were sold off during the 1860s, but deceased Savannah residents continue to be buried in Laurel Grove South today.

QUICK BREAK

Laurel Grove is a short drive from the Victorian and Starland Districts. For coffee or a light lunch, try **Foxy Coffee**. There's also many choices at **Starland Yard Tood Truck Park** (p138).

EXPERIENCES

Start a Tab at Starland Yard

FOOD TRUCKS

Whoa, whoa, whoa – don't speed-walk into this eye-catching **food truck park** (MAP: 1 P134 **A5**; *starlandyard.com*), housed within a collection of shipping containers. You've got to stop and swipe your credit card at the entrance station, which allows you to order whatever you want and simply pay when you leave. All your orders, no matter the vendor, are connected to the same register. The entrance pay station is a great concept, as is the variety of tasty fare on offer here. Options include pizza, Mexican dishes and sandwiches, and there's a bar serving a slew of regional beers. A few additional food trucks may also pull up daily. Check the Starland Yard website for an up-to-date list.

If you're with a group, try the delicious wood-fired pizzas from **Vittoria Pizzeria** (MAP: 2 P134 **A4**) – the spicy La Diavola is divine. **Open-mic poetry** in Starland Yard is on Monday night and **music bingo** is on Sunday night.

Tour the Savannah African Art Museum

MUSEUM

MAP: 3 P134 **G4**

You'll join a tour to explore the treasures displayed at this privately owned **museum** *(savannahafricanartmuseum.org; free)*, which showcases 19th- and 20th-century spiritual and ceremonial art objects from 28 African countries in West and Central Africa. Year-long temporary exhibits have covered everything from the traditions associated with textiles to the importance of cowrie shells. **Tours** *(11am-4pm Wed-Sat)* begin every hour and half hour, and cover either West or Central Africa.

Gallery Hop on First Friday

ART WALK

MAP: 4 P134 **B5**

For a cluster of creativity, and definitely some craft beer and cocktails, make your way to the **First Friday art walk** *(5-9pm)* in Starland, a collaborative neighborhood event that sees local galleries, shops and breweries keep their doors open late on the first Friday of the month. Pop-up vendors and live music, as well as drinks and snacks, add to the fun. Events might include short films, karaoke, workshops and artist takeovers. Galleries cluster near DeSoto Ave and Bull and Dayton Sts. Visit @starlandfirstfridays on Instagram for the full list of participating businesses.

Appreciate Local Creativity

GALLERIES

MAP: 5 P134 **B4**

Arts Southeast *(artssoutheast.org)*, a nonprofit organization supporting emerging local artists, oversees several galleries and exhibition spaces in Starland. Its flagship is **Sulfur Studios**, an art showplace that is home to the Ellis

Gallery, 26 artist studios and the **Sulfur Shop**, which sells original works as well as ceramics, jewelry, prints and notecards. Arts Southeast also curates the **Drive Thru Art Box**, a tiny art space tucked inside a former drive-thru menu box at **Green Truck Pub**. Exhibits can be quite creative!

Watch the Savannah Bananas

BASEBALL

MAP: 6 P134 **H6**

There's baseball – and then there are the **Savannah Bananas** *(thesavannahbananas.com; tickets $35-100)*. Think of the Harlem Globetrotters, but imagine baseball players instead of basketball. The Bananas and other teams in the Banana League play by 'banana ball' rules, which keep games fast and entertaining. Every inning in this exhibition league is worth one point, and games are capped at two hours.

Savannah Banana players wear kilts and perform choreographed dances – and it's all part of the fun. Their season lasts about nine months and the team plays in Savannah about once or twice per month. Games are at Grayson Stadium in **Daffin Park** on E Victory Dr in the Midtown neighborhood east of Starland. Games are extremely popular, so you'll need to enter a lottery on the website – which closes the fall before the following year's season – to get tickets.

Take a Cooking Class with Chef Darin

CLASS

MAP: 7 P134 **G6**

When you tire of eating all that sinful Southern food (OK, that may never happen), try your hand at making it – along with dishes from other cuisines – in a **cooking class** *(chefdarin.com; classes $85-100)* with local top chef Darin Sehnert. His theme-driven classes include Low Country Cuisine, French Bistro and Northern Italian. Most run about 3½ hours. There's also a store stocked with fine kitchen accoutrements.

SOUL FOOD

When it comes to perceptions of cuisine from this part of the country, the distinction between Southern food and soul food can be blurry. While all soul food is Southern food, not all Southern food is soul – the roots of the latter stem from what was developed by enslaved Africans in the Southeastern United States as they made do with whatever was available to them. Traditional dishes include fried chicken and fish, ham hocks, oxtails, chitlins, pigs' feet, hush puppies and greens (collard, mustard or turnip). These parallel with a lot of Southern foods, though the soul variety is often fattier, saltier and spicier.

Sip a Sour Beer at Two Tides Brewing Co BREWERY

MAP: 8 P134 A5

The 'door' to the 2nd-floor balcony at **Two Tides** *(twotidesbrewing.com)* is a window – just slide it up toward the ceiling and step outside. The window is just one of the many quirky charms at this small brewery, which occupies the upper floor of a two-story building that's a bit of a hybrid – upstairs is a house dating to the early 1900s, while the lower level was transformed into a commercial space once used by Starland Dairy (where the neighborhood gets its name).

Owned by husband-and-wife team James and Liz Massey, Two Tides is welcoming and completely free of attitude. Solo travelers will feel comfortable here. If you're part of a small group, arrive early to explore the warren of rooms behind the taproom. The beer list is adventurous and tasty, with an emphasis on sours, haze and funk. The brewery also serves coffee. You'll find a cocktail bar downstairs, and a permanent food truck, **Crispi**, parked out front and serving up smashburgers.

Shopping in Starland SHOPPING

With its murals, candy-colored storefronts and evocatively named businesses, Starland can be a tough place to stay focused. The shops near Starland Yard in particular pop like an Instagram feed come to life.

You might feel as though you're being watched while you flip through the vinyl inside **Graveface Records & Curiosities** (MAP: 9 P134 B5; *graveface.com*). Just blame it on the taxidermy and figurines. And maybe that Fiji merman on the shelf. Despite the quirkiness, this is a refreshingly welcoming record store. Around the corner you can sip a latte while browsing jewelry and gifts at super-cute **Superbloom** (MAP: 10 P134 B5; *superbloomsav.com*). Savannah-themed T-shirts and Dolly Parton stickers are highlights in **Starland Strange & Bazaar** (MAP: 11 P134 A6; *starlandstrangeandbazaar.com*). The shop also sells ice cream. Artists can buy new and reclaimed art supplies at rainbow-bright **Starlandia Supply** (MAP: 12 P134 C5; *starlandiasupply.com*) on Bull St.

Bull St is the main artery running through these neighborhoods, which are south of the Historic District. Laurel Grove Cemetery is the sight furthest west, just at the edge of the Victorian District. Daffin Park, where the Savannah Bananas play home games, is all the way east down Victory Dr just before you approach East Savannah. Most sights, such as the Starland Yard area right in the center, are easy to navigate on foot; beyond that, a car or bike is the way to roll within the neighborhoods.

Best Places for...

See p134 for map of locations

$ Budget $$ Midrange $$$ Top End

Eating

Breakfast

Narobia's Grits & Gravy $
13 H4
Lovers of soul food, seafood and breakfast food will get their fill with the simple, hearty plates at this humble hole in the wall. The French toast and crab biscuit are not to be missed. *7am-noon Tue-Fri, 8am-1pm Sat*

Big Bon Bodega $
14 F4
Stop in for fresh bagels and a creative list of bagel sandwiches. The Pimento Pig is stuffed with sausage, egg and pimento cheddar. *7am-7pm Wed-Sat*

Modern American

Local11Ten $$$
15 H1
Upscale, sustainable, local and fresh: these elements help create an elegant, well-run restaurant that's one of Savannah's best. In the Victorian District. *5:30-9pm Wed-Sun*

Comfort Food

Green Truck Pub $
16 H6
Casual pub serving locally sourced and house-made fare. Its burgers are the best in town – try the Trailer Park, adorned with pimento cheese and bacon. *11:30am-10pm Mon-Sat*

Brochu's $
17 C5
New on the scene, this neighborhood joint in Starland has quickly earned acclaim for its oh-so-tasty fried chicken. Serves cocktails too. *5-9pm Wed, Thu & Sun, to 10pm Fri & Sat*

Coffee

Sentient Bean
19 H1
Longtime favorite across the street from the south entrance to Forsyth Park. Start here before walking to the Saturday morning farmers market. *7am-7pm*

Foxy Loxy Cafe
 F3
Buzzing cafe and art-print gallery in an old Victorian house that's usually full of students and creatives. The courtyard out back is the loveliest in this area. It serves tasty tacos and freshly baked *kolaches* (fruit pastries). *8am-9pm Mon-Sat, to 6pm Sun*

Drinking

Bars

Wormhole
18 B4
Locally loved watering hole in Starland hosting live bands, comedy, DJs, trivia, open mic, karaoke and more. There's pool, darts and video games too, plus a full menu of food until late. *noon-3am*

Shopping

Antiques

Picker Joe's Antique Mall
21 G6
Pickin' and siftin' for treasures is a delight in this bright, organized mall that was once a mattress factory. *10am-6pm Mon-Sat, noon-5pm Sun*

See p159
for eating,
drinking and
shopping
listings

Explore
East Savannah & the Islands

Expansive marshlands and winding estuaries slip into the sea in East Savannah, the more tranquil side of the city – with the exception of Tybee Island, where locals love a wacky parade. Great seafood and scenery await, from the city's eastern edge and the riverside township of Thunderbolt, home to Bonaventure Cemetery, past the residential enclaves of Whitemarsh and Talahi Islands. You'll feel your cares drop away as you swoop over the glowing marsh grasses that fringe the road all the way to Tybee Island, home to eclectic art shops, laid-back cafes and pretty beaches.

Getting Around

Car

There's only one way on and off these islands. US Hwy 80 threads them all together, starting on the eastern side of Savannah on Victory Dr, which eventually turns into Butler Ave on Tybee.

Bike

Cycling is easy on Tybee Island, which has bike paths linking its northern and southern ends, which are 3 miles apart. Follow the paths on Bay St and Chatham Ave.

Golf Cart

Golf carts zip around Tybee Island. Rent one at Coast to Coast Beach Rentals *(coasttocoasttybee.com)*, which also has e-bikes.

Skidaway Island State Park (p157)

DOUGLAS RISSING/GETTY IMAGES ©

THE BEST

SOUTHERN GOTHIC MOOD Bonaventure Cemetery (p146)

HISTORIC SITE Wormsloe State Historic Site (p150)

CULTURE Pin Point Heritage Museum (p154)

BEACH North Beach (p156)

AFTERNOON HANG Sea Wolf (p153)

A
B
C
D
1
2
3
4
5
6
Islands Expwy
Oatland Island
McQueens Island
Pennsylvania Ave
Bee Rd
Harry S Truman Pkwy
12
Bonaventure Rd
Shannon Scott Tours
Bonaventure Cemetery
80
E Victory Dr
Thunderbolt
Talahi Island
Bryan Woods Rd
Whatley Ave
Skidaway Rd
Jasmine Ave
E Derenne Ave
Whitemarsh Island
Johnny Mercer Blvd
Walthour Rd
Herb River
Skidaway River
Howard Foss Dr
La Roche Ave
Winchester Dr
Walthour Rd
Wilmington Island Rd
11
Isle of Hope
Comus Dr
Skidaway Rd
Sister Island
Halfmoon River
Wormsloe Historic Site
Pin Point Heritage Museum
5
Skidaway Island State Park
McWhorter Dr
Cabbage Island
Wilmington River
204
Diamond Causeway
Skidaway Island
GEORGIA
Landings Way
Wassaw Island
Wassaw National Wildlife Refuge

For more see

Top Experiences p146
Experiences p156
Eating p159
Drinking p159
Shopping p159

★ TOP EXPERIENCE

Bonaventure Cemetery

A lush necropolis on the banks of the Wilmington River, Bonaventure is one of the world's most beautiful cemeteries. The Southern Gothic tombs and monuments, set against a 100-acre natural landscape awash with ferns, azaleas, dwarf palmettos and Spanish-moss-riddled live oaks, conjure a serene reverence that's just the right kind of haunting.

MAP P144 **B1**

PLANNING TIP
The Bonaventure Historical Society Visitor Center *(10am-4pm Sat & Sun)* at the entrance sells a helpful illustrated cemetery map *($8)*.

Scan this QR code for further information.

Famous Burials

Bonaventure was the final stop for many well-known Savannahians. Among the most famous grave sites is that of 'Little Gracie' Watson, a six-year-old local girl who died in 1889. Her father had a sculptor carve a detailed life-size statue of her from a photograph shortly before the family moved away from Savannah. To this day, visitors bring toys, flowers and other trinkets to her grave. Her grave site is located in Section E, Lot 98.

The cemetery is also home to the grave sites of Great American Songbook–era musician Johnny Mercer (pictured p148), whose family plot features a bench inscribed with lyrics from the singer's works, and Pulitzer Prize–winning poet Conrad Aiken. Mercer's grave is located in Section H, Lot 48, while Aiken's grave is located a few steps away, closer to the river, in Section H, Lot 78.

Bonaventure in Pop Culture

Bonaventure's beauty became known to the world with John Berendt's best-selling nonfiction novel and film *Midnight in the Garden of Good and Evil* (1994). Characters in the book visit the cemetery and gossip over martinis at the grave

NATOE/SHUTTERSTOCK ©

site of poet Conrad Aiken, where a bench takes the place of a headstone. Scenes from the film, directed by Clint Eastwood, were also shot at the cemetery.

The famous *Midnight* cover features a statue of the *Bird Girl*, which sat virtually unnoticed until 1993, when Random House commissioned local photographer Jack Leigh for an image. After two days of searching for a subject, Leigh quickly captured the photo as dusk approached, then spent 10 hours in the darkroom developing it. The result was an eerie creation that appears awash in moonlight, and it became one of the most iconic photographs ever taken in Savannah. The statue became so popular from the success of the book that it was removed from Bonaventure and now sits on display in the Telfair Academy (p126).

QUICK BREAK

If you're in the mood for a picnic, Bonaventure has a handful of tables by the river. Sisters of the New South (p159) is a convenient pick if you'd like a little soul food after exploring the grounds.

BONAVENTURE BLOG

For updates about specialty tours, lectures, dedications and remembrance days, check the Bonaventure Historical Society's blog at bonaventure historical.org.

Cemetery Night Tour

For extra atmosphere, join **Shannon Scott Tours** *(shannonscotttours.com; tour $45)* for its *Bonaventure Cemetery After Hours Tour*, led by local historian Shannon Scott. The two-hour tour is the only way to see the cemetery at night, offering a different perspective on the history, architecture and traditions of Savannah's alluring city of the dead. Note that the tour is suitable for those 18 years and up.

Cemetery Etiquette

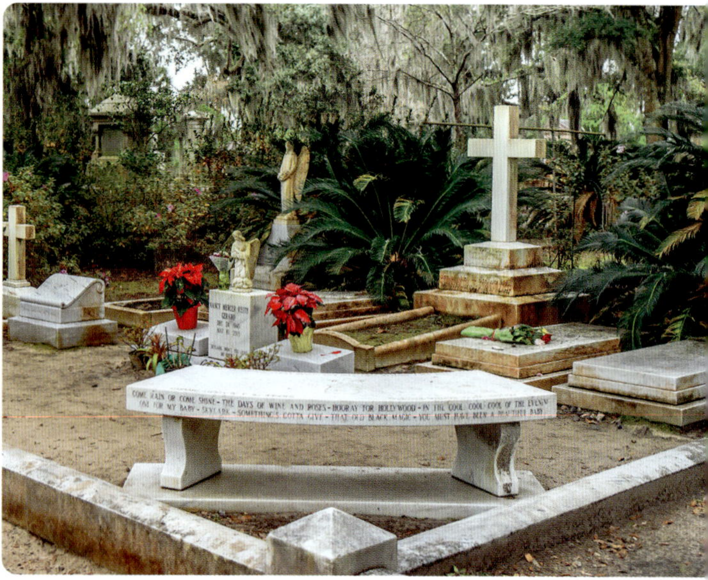

Bonaventure is a beautiful place, but it's also a working cemetery and a sacred spot that is often visited by those who are grieving. The historical society has a few guidelines for visitors. Most importantly, if you see a hearse and a small crowd, that is likely a funeral, and private. Remember to keep your voices low.

Before you arrive, it's worth reminding children to remain respectful for the duration of your visit. Park in designated areas and do not block cemetery roads. Do not idle your car, which can harm headstones. The cemetery is city-owned, but the plots are privately owned, so if you stray onto a plot for that perfect shot or up-close view, you are technically trespassing. Do not stand on stones or touch headstones. Leashed pets are permitted on the cemetery grounds.

Exploring the Cemetery

The **Bonaventure Cemetery Historical Society website** *(bonaventurehistorical.org)* shares helpful information about visiting the cemetery. For more details about those buried here, consider a guided or self-guided tour. The historical society also runs a free **tour** *(2pm Sat & Sun 2nd weekend of month)*. Its Bonaventure Cemetery Tour **app** *($6)* includes 23 stops.

John Muir Slept Here

During a hiking excursion through several eastern states in 1867, John Muir stopped in Savannah. Originally from Scotland, the future writer and conservationist ended up staying six days in the city. With only $1.50 on hand, he decided to spend several nights in Bonaventure – no lodging fees here! He gave the cemetery the 19th-century equivalent of a five-star review in his journal: 'The rippling living waters, the song of birds, the joyous confidence of flowers, the calm, undisturbable grandeur of the oaks, mark this place of graves as one of the Lord's most favored abodes of life and light.'

VICTORIAN SYMBOLS

During the Victorian era (1837–1901) many cemeteries and gravesites in America and England began adding sculptures, gardens, ornate grave markers and symbolic features. These additions reflected a more romantic view of death. Bonaventure is no exception, and you'll find mortuary sculptures of angels, cherubs, couches and beds, as well as benches and Egyptian obelisks – representing eternal life – dotting the landscape.

★ TOP EXPERIENCE

Wormsloe State Historic Site

A majestic corridor of live oak trees stretches across this **colonial estate**, developed by one of Georgia's original European settlers. The first plantation established by the British in the colony, it has served as a military stronghold, a country residence and a farm.

MAP: P144 **A4**

GETTING THERE
Wormsloe is on the Isle of Hope in the Moon River District southeast of Savannah. Follow Victory Dr east from Savannah to Skidaway Rd for about 10 miles. The entrance is on the right.

Scan this QR code for more information.

Wormsloe's Establishment

Noble Jones, a carpenter, came to Savannah with Georgia founder James Oglethorpe in 1733. Thanks to Oglethorpe's friendship with Yamacraw tribe chief Tomochichi, the uninhabited land that would become Wormsloe was amicably acquired from the native tribe, and in 1737, four years after Savannah was established, the Isle of Hope peninsula was granted to three of the early colonizers. Noble Jones was among them, and he obtained a lease of 500 acres that would eventually form the core of the site.

Strategic Defense

After establishing itself in Florida in the previous century, Spain retained loose control over the Georgia coast throughout the late 17th century thanks to its Native American allies. This brought the Spanish into conflict with the English colonies in the Carolinas. The Spanish missions off the Georgia coast were subsequently destroyed, rendering the largely abandoned area a buffer zone between the Spanish and the English. When the English chose to colonize the land between Florida and South Carolina – prompting the arrival of Oglethorpe in

OLGA V KULAKOVA/SHUTTERSTOCK ©

1733 – there was concern that the Spanish would attempt to oust them.

Sure enough, conflict broke out with the War of Jenkins' Ear. Wormsloe's strategic location on the Isle of Hope peninsula gave it a valuable role in defending the colony from Spanish attacks from the south. On his 500-acre plot, Jones constructed a fortified house of wood and tabby (a crude concrete composed of oyster shells and lime mortar). The five-room, 1½-story house featured 8ft ceilings and bastions on all four corners, and was one of several protective outposts along Georgia's chain of barrier islands.

Exploring Wormsloe

Stop by the **visitor center** *(9am-4:45pm)* to buy admission tickets and pick up a property map. You'll also board the tram that shuttles between the visitor center and the park museum via **Live**

QUICK BREAK
Hidden along an estuary of the Savannah marshlands, laid-back **Wyld** *(thewylddockbar.com)* offers a seasonal New American menu with a seafood emphasis. It's also an ace spot to catch live music and chill in a hammock.

COLONIAL FAIRE & MUSTER
Wormsloe hosts a living history weekend every March during the statewide **Georgia History Festival** *(georgiahistory.com).*

Oak Avenue, which was originally flanked by more than 400 moss-draped oaks. About 75 or so have been lost over the years. Your shuttle guide will share a few facts about the property along the way. If you want to immerse yourself in their beauty and take scads of photos, you can walk the length of the oak alley. Just be aware that the trees may lose a little luster on a humid afternoon if you're walking – it's a 1.5-mile walk one way!

From the museum it's a short stroll to the ruins of the original **tabby house** (pictured). Dating from 1745, these are the oldest European-built ruins in Georgia. From here, walk to the **Jones family grave site** and the **Colonial Life Area**, where interpreters in period costumes may be on hand to demonstrate Colonial-era crafting and toolwork.

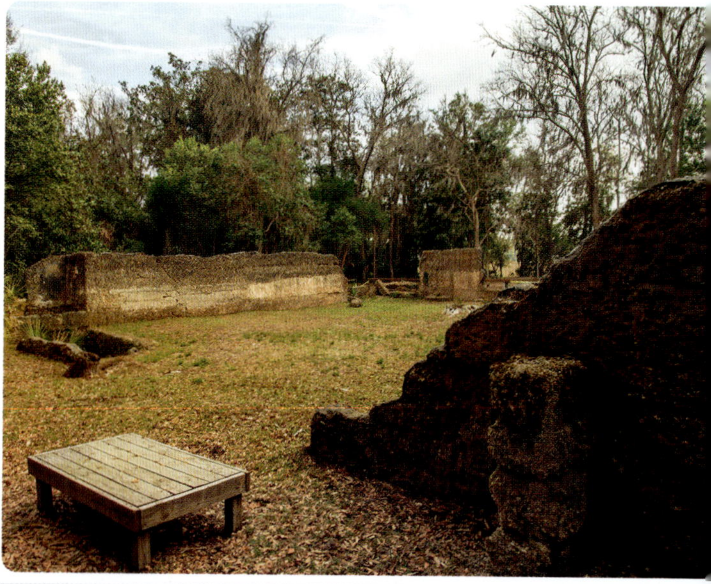

An **observation deck** near the Colonial Life Area overlooks a pretty stretch of marsh. In the 1700s, before it became clogged with silt, there was a channel here that was an important waterway for ships. Listen carefully as you stand on the observation deck. Hear that popping sound? Those are pistol shrimp in the marsh snapping their claws, pistol style! The sound is so loud it actually stuns their prey – and it confounds city folk who pause by the marsh.

Battlements & a Dairy

Near the museum you can follow the 2.5-mile **Battery Trail** through the forest to the banks of the Moon River and see Battery Wymberly. These Confederate military fortifications were used during the Civil War. Ask for a detailed trail map at the museum.

Forty acres of private property – an 1828 plantation house and a **dairy** – border the eastern flank of the oak alley. Descendants of Noble Jones – the family's eighth generation! – live on the property. You can trace their family tree in the museum. The family opened the property to visitors in 1927, and it was acquired by the state in 1973.

What's in a Name?

Noble Jones named his Isle of Hope estate 'Wormslow,' which was likely a nod to Wormslow Hundred in Herefordshire, the county on the Wales border that was the Jones family homeland. Some suggest that the name is a reference to Jones' efforts to cultivate silkworms on the plantation – but since the plantation was named 'Lambeth,' after the London borough that Jones was born in, the former theory is probably correct.

TOP TIPS

For a dramatic photo of the Avenue of the Oaks in cooler, damper weather, visit first thing in the morning before the fog dissipates. On historic dates or holiday weekends, check for special events with costumed demonstrations of colonial-era skills and traditions. Guided tours are offered regularly. Call 912-353-3023 for times. Reservations are recommended.

★ TOP EXPERIENCE

Pin Point Heritage Museum

Occupying the former AS Varn & Son Oyster Seafood Factory beside a marshy stretch of the Moon River, this museum spotlights the culture of the Gullah-Geechee people in the secluded Pin Point community, which was established by first-generation formerly enslaved and thrived for nearly 100 years.

MAP: P144 **A5**

GETTING THERE
You'll need to drive to Pin Point, which is located in the Moon River District about 12 miles from downtown Savannah. For more history, consider visiting the nearby Wormsloe Historic Site (p150).

Scan this QR code for further information.

Movie & Museum

Crab pickers worked their dexterous magic inside the **Picking & Cooling House**, which now holds a museum and a tiny movie room showing the documentary *Take Me to the Water*. With its gorgeous footage of the languid marshes, the film is visually compelling, but it's the memories and stories shared by former residents – among them Supreme Court justice Clarence Thomas – that will stay with you.

Exhibits in the **museum** *(9am-4pm, Thu-Sat)* trace the history of the community, touching on its Native American heritage, the arrival of enslaved West Africans, the growth of Gullah-Geechee culture and the role of AS Varn & Son as a community anchor. The factory was in operation from 1926 to 1985, and today about 300 people live in the community.

Plan to spend an hour to 90 minutes at the site.

Oyster Factory & Crab Boiling Pavilion

You can almost hear the clack of falling oyster shells inside the **Oyster House**, where women would shuck the oysters brought in on flat-bottomed marsh boats, known as bateaux. You can see

TRISHA PING/LONELY PLANET ©

their work stations, learn their stories and check out an actual bateau.

During crab season older boys would boil blue crabs in giant pots in the factory's open-air **pavilion**. They would leave them in the Picking & Cooling House to cool off before being picked the next day by the women.

Beauty by the Marsh

Take a moment to soak up the graceful beauty of the salt marsh and adjacent Moon River. Docents with ties to the Pin Point community are available to answer your questions at picnic tables beside the marsh after the movie or while you explore the factory buildings. Take a moment to ask them about the stories and history connected with this special place.

QUICK BREAK

If you're craving barbecue, drive 3 miles to cozy **Sandfly BBQ** for minced pork sandwiches. For soul food, step up to the counter at Sisters of the New South (p159), serving delicious collards and fried chicken.

EXPERIENCES

Cross the Moat into Fort Pulaski

FORT

MAP: 1 P144 **G2**

As you cross its deep moat and walk through the 22ft-high walls that protect it, **Fort Pulaski** *(nps.gov/fopu; adult/child $10/ free)* looks impenetrable. But looks are deceiving.

Completed in 1847 on a prime defensive spot on Cockspur Island at the mouth of the Savannah River, the fort was considered invincible. As US Chief of Engineers General Totten proclaimed, 'You might as well bombard the Rocky Mountains.' Unfortunately for the Confederates, who occupied the fort at the start of the Civil War, Union forces were in possession of a new weapon: rifled guns. On April 10, 1862, they trained these powerful weapons on the garrison from Tybee Island and began to fire. After just 30 hours of bombardment, the walls of Fort Pulaski were heavily damaged and pocked with smoking holes. The guns atop the fort's ramparts were also destroyed. The Confederates realized the hopelessness of their position and surrendered on April 11.

Rangers share more details inside the fort, and you can easily envision the siege while strolling the ramparts and parade grounds. It's a surprisingly fascinating place. Beyond the fort you can hike short trails that crisscross the park grounds.

Hike the McQueen's Island Historic Trail

TRAIL

MAP: 2 P144 **E1**

The 6-mile **McQueen's Island Historic Trail** begins just outside the entrance to Fort Pulaski National Monument. This county-run trail, built along an old railroad bed, is open for walking and cycling. The trail parallels the south channel of the Savannah River. From the trail, scan for box turtles, red-tailed hawks and brown pelicans.

Spend a Day on the Sand at North Beach

BEACH

MAP: 3 P144 **H2**

There's a bit of a walk from the parking lot to **North Beach**, but the extended stroll does add to the sense of anticipation. And the payoff – a beautiful swath of white sand – is worth it. With fewer services and a vibe that feels more remote, this stretch of beach is a great place to relax. You can also watch massive container ships drift in from the sea, especially if you take a left once you hit the sand and walk north up the shore to the point where the Savannah River runs into the Atlantic.

Beachcombing is also good along North Beach. Keep an eye out for fossilized shark teeth in the sand as you walk. The North Beach area is also a recommended spot for bird-watching.

Tybee Island Light Station & Museum

LIGHTHOUSE

MAP: 4 P144 **H2**

Everything seems fine as you huff and puff up the 178-step staircase that corkscrews to the top of the **Tybee Island Light Station** *(tybeelighthouse.org; adult/child $12/10)* – until you reach the fourth-level platform and its complimentary barf bags, which hang on the wall. The graphic barfing emoji on the bag is a bit of a buzzkill, but no matter. There are numerous windows to break up the climb, and the view of the coast grows prettier as you ascend. Once at the top you'll enjoy panoramic views of the island from the observation deck.

Tickets include admission to the adjacent lighthouse keeper's cottage and **museum**. Tybee Light Station is the 20th-highest lighthouse in the US, soaring 145ft. The lighthouse is closed on Tuesday.

Embrace Nature on Little Tybee Island

ISLAND

MAP: 6 P144 **G4**

An uninhabited barrier island, **Little Tybee Island** is only accessible by boat or kayak. Located just south of Tybee Island, it's actually double its size. The preserved land is rich with coastal marshland, dunes, wildlife and subtropical forests and is a great place to camp. Kayaking the marshes is another highlight. There aren't any facilities on the island, but there's no fee and you can visit any time. Experienced kayakers can rent from any of the outfitters around Tybee, or you can book a charter service that runs trips to the island.

BEST FOR BIRD-WATCHING

Skidaway Island State Park

MAP: 5 P144 **A5**

Home to maritime forest, marshes and a tidal creek, this state park hosts herons, egrets and bald eagles year-round.

Fort Pulaski National Monument

see 1 **G2**

Walk through marshlands, open fields and soaring pines and look for painted buntings and salt-marsh sparrows.

Little Tybee Island

see 6 **G4**

This undeveloped island and nature preserve is only accessible by boat.

Party Like a Pirate on Tybee Island

EVENT

Don your best pirate outfit and prepare to swill mugs of grog in mid-October, when Tybee Island throws its annual **Pirate Fest** *(tybeepiratefest.com)*. During this weekend-long festival you can dance at the Buccaneer Ball, join a pirate pub crawl, browse the Thieves Market and participate in

BEST ANNUAL EVENTS

Tybee Island Beach Bum Parade
Started in 1987, this parade is a giant traveling water fight. Come prepared with a water gun – no one is safe! Held in mid-May.

Tybee Turtle Trot
This 5km beach run is a fundraiser for turtle-preservation efforts, and it coincides with sea-turtle nesting season. Held in late April.

Pirate Fest
This four-day festival in mid-October celebrates the pirate life. Dress up like your favorite buccaneer and get ready to party like it's 1699.

all sorts of pirate mayhem. Other distractions include live music, a parade and, well, bouncy houses – don't enter with your sword. The festival kicked off in 2005.

Enjoy the Arts in Tybee

PERFORMING ARTS

MAP: 7 P144 **H2**

Tybee might be small, but residents celebrate the arts in a big way, with many events taking place at the **Tybee Post Theater**, constructed in 1930 as a movie house for army soldiers. It went dark in the '60s and dodged the wrecking ball at the turn of the century. Now the landmark has been reborn as a concert hall, cultural and educational performance venue, theater and film-screening stage. Check the theater's Facebook page *(facebook.com/TybeePostTheater)* for the most up-to-date event schedule.

Join the Action at Tybee Pier & Pavilion

BEACH

MAP: 8 P144 **H3**

The **pier** and the adjacent pavilion are Tybee's primary beachside hub, with a large parking lot, public bathrooms, concessions and a long fishing pier. Tables in the pavilion are available to rent by the hour.

Best Places for...

$ Budget $$ Midrange $$$ Top End

Eating

Seafood

Sea Wolf $

9 H2

Slurp oysters and snarf down some darn-fine messy hotdogs on the laid-back patio. Add a breeze, a cocktail and a couple of guys on guitar, and it approaches perfection. On Tybee Island. *4-10pm Mon-Fri, 11am-10pm Sat & Sun*

Crab Shack $$

10 H2

This hidden favorite on Tybee Island slings bountiful peel-and-eat seafood platters in a multishack complex alongside an alligator lagoon. *11:30am-9pm*

Castaways $$

 A3

The colorful nautical murals put paid to the strip-mall setting at this seafood joint near Wormsloe. *11am-9pm Sun-Thu, to 10pm Fri & Sat*

Southern US

Sisters of the New South $

12 A1

This laid-back cafe in the Moon River District serves hearty Southern soul-food favorites. The red-velvet cake will knock your socks off. Order at the counter. *11am-9pm Mon-Thu, to 9:30pm Fri-Sun*

Sundae Cafe at Tybee $$$

13 H3

Clean up nice and treat yourself to exquisitely prepared seafood and steak dishes with a Southern spin at this buzzing cafe in a former ice-cream parlor. Reservations recommended. *4-9pm Mon-Sat*

Drinking

Coffee

Tybean Coffee Bar

 H2

Step into the cheerful turquoise shack in the Shops at Tybee in the North Beach area for espresso drinks, cold brew coffee and frappés. *7:30am-1pm*

Shopping

Art & Craft

Shops at Tybee Oaks

see 14 H2

As you cruise over the bridge and land on Tybee, clusters of adorable indie shops immediately beckon on your left. You'll find pottery, art and beachwear in the the dozen shops at Tybee Oaks.

Shoppes at 1207

see 14 H2

The Tybee Art Gallery is one of four pastel cottages here, a short walk from the Shops at Tybee Oaks. Hosts fun shopping events the Cookie Crawl and the Pajama Rama – shop in your pjs!

Charleston & Savannah Toolkit

Hilton Head (p99)

ROADPIX/ALAMY STOCK PHOTO ©

Family Travel

Charleston and Savannah are imaginative cities, and they're fun places to bring kids of all ages, with plenty of attractions, museums and parks. Several wide beaches, with playgrounds and seasonal lifeguards, are nearby.

Is the Lowcountry Good for Kids?

Though Charleston and Savannah are famous romantic destinations, there are plenty of activities for kids and families. The South Carolina Aquarium (p64) and the Old Exchange & Provost Dungeon (p45) are entertaining options in Charleston, while children's museums and ghost tours are highlights in Savannah. It's also easy to get out on the rivers and marshes, which are a short drive from the cities.

SPLASH PADS

Charleston County Parks manages three seasonal water parks. **Scan the QR code to find one nearby.**

SK8 Charleston

If you have skateboarders in the family, check out **SK8 Charleston**, a 32,500-sq-ft skate park just north of NoMo that overlooks the Ashley River. Skaters can tackle a 200ft snake run, a pro bowl, an intermediate bowl and a 315ft street course. There's also live music, concessions and a skate shop. Also offers lessons.

Older Kids

Boat tours and guided kayaking trips are abundant. Join a tour to look for wildlife, learn local history and add a bit of adventure.

Free & Easy Transportation

For short trips, hop aboard the DASH shuttle in Charleston or the DOT express shuttle in Savannah.

Take a Walk

Historic house tours may be of little interest to younger kids. Instead, stroll the historic neighborhoods, pointing out gardens and monuments. Busy riverfronts are captivating too, with large container ships passing just offshore.

Accommodations

From revamped motor courts to swish boutique hotels, Charleston and Savannah have a wide range of lodging options. Prices tend to be steeper in the popular historic districts.

Where to Stay if You Love...

History & Famous Restaurants

South of Broad & the French Quarter (p37)
Chef-driven restaurants and historic homes are steps from trendy hotels and well-loved inns in Charleston. Expect high prices and afternoon wine hours.

OUR PICK

We Love to Stay in...

Historic & Power Plant Districts (p115)
Hospitality and history abound in this centuries-old Savannah neighborhood, where an evening walk includes Gothic town squares, ghost tours, convivial restaurants and folks enjoying open-container laws. Rooftop patios and a vibrant riverfront scene add to the charm.

Museums & Local Eats

East Side, NoMo & Hampton Park (p49)
Learn the story of Charleston at top-notch museums. Chain hotels and glossy boutiques are close to popular neighborhood bars and eateries.

HOW MUCH FOR A NIGHT IN

Revamped motor court **from $120**

Independent inn **from $200**

Downtown boutique hotel **from $330**

Beach Towns & Watersports

Charleston County Sea Islands (p79)
Families and beachcombers enjoy quick access to wide sandy beaches. Lodging options include cottages, motels and swanky resorts.

Quirky Locals & Gorgeous Beaches

East Savannah & the Islands (p143) Hop on a golf cart to scoot around Tybee Island, where locals love a party. Spend the night in rental cottages and mom-and-pop inns and hotels.

Sea Island Views & Boat Cruises

Beaufort and Hilton Head (p99) Historic Beaufort is a small-town launchpad for exploring Gullah-Geechee culture, while Hilton Head is a well-manicured barrier island with oodles of amenities.

Food, Drink & Nightlife

Allergies & Intolerances

Visitors with food allergies and intolerances will have few difficulties dining out. Substances that could trigger a reaction, such as nuts and gluten, are often listed on menus, and servers are typically well trained in answering questions about food issues. Be sure to communicate your allergy clearly to your server, however. Note that seafood is commonly found on menus across the Lowcountry.

FROGMORE STEW

A Lowcountry boil, also known as Frogmore stew, is a bowl of shell-on shrimp, corn on the cob, sausage and red potatoes boiled or steamed together.

JAMES BEARD WINNERS

Numerous chefs and restaurants in Charleston and Savannah have been recognized for their culinary prowess by the James Beard Foundation. Notable winners in Charleston include **FIG** (p68) and **Rodney Scott's BBQ** (p65). Mashama Bailey, the driving force behind Savannah's **The Grey** (p128), won Best Chef: Southeast in 2019 and Outstanding Chef in 2022.

Lowcountry Favorites

Shrimp and grits is arguably the Lowcountry's most famous dish, enjoyed in varying preparations across the region. She-crab soup – named for its crab-roe garnish – is another regional favorite. Buttermilk biscuits are delicious with a bit of butter, but they also come smothered in gravy or piled with pimento cheese.

Pay the Bill

If your waiter or waitress doesn't bring the bill, it's OK to request it when you're ready to leave. Just catch their eye and nod that you're ready.

Splitting the bill is usually not an issue, unless you're in a large group. In that case give your server a heads-up before the table starts ordering.

A tip is not typically included in the bill, although it may be automatically added for larger groups, usually six or more. Otherwise, a tip of 18% to 25% is standard and expected at restaurants.

PRICE RANGES

The following price ranges refer to the average cost of a main course:

$ less than $15

$$ $15–25

$$$ more than $25

OPENING HOURS

Bars 3pm to 3am, from noon on Saturday

Clubs 9pm to 3am

Restaurants 6am to 11am (breakfast), 11am to around 3pm (lunch and weekend brunch) and 5pm to 11pm (dinner)

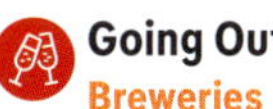

Going Out

Breweries

Charleston's brewery scene is booming, and you'll find festive crowds gathering for a pint after work and on weekends at their neighborhood favorite. Most breweries are found outside the Historic District, closer to North Charleston and across the sea islands.

Cocktail bars The historic areas of Charleston and Savannah are best known for their craft cocktail bars. Find them inside hotels or in cozy enclaves tucked into alleyways.

Rooftop bars Stylish rooftop bars seem to open monthly, and you'll find them across both cities. The most popular may require a reservation on weekend nights. The vibe is more welcoming than in other metropolitan areas, but to fit in you may want to check the dress code or wear your cleanest dirty shirt.

Live music Singer-song-writers energize crowds on sunny afternoons at restaurants, microbreweries and distilleries in Charleston and Savannah. Touring regional bands often stop at The Refinery (p66) and the Pour House (p94) in the Charleston area.

HOW MUCH FOR A

Drip coffee
from $2.60

Specialty coffee
from $3

Craft beer
$6–7

Glass of wine
from $11

Cocktail
from $16

Cup of she-crab soup
$10

Barbecue sandwich
$16

Shrimp and grits
from $27

LGBTIQ+ Travelers

South Carolina and Georgia are socially conservative states, but Charleston and Savannah are welcoming to the LGBTIQ+ community. Both have healthy cultural scenes, although Savannah's is more active.

Pride Events

Held in late October to avoid the summer heat, the two-day **Savannah Pride Celebration** *(savannahpridecenter.org)* brings music, art and good vibes to Forsyth Park (p118). The event celebrated its 25th anniversary in 2024. Each year a theme such as 'Barbie in the Park' triggers a slew of creative costumes.

Held in mid-September, **Charleston Pride** *(charlestonpride.org)* fills an entire week, with popular bars and music venues hosting events like Drag Bingo and Queer Kickball. In 2024 the The Refinery (p66) hosted the week-capping **Charleston Pride Festival**, celebrating the LGBTIQ+ community with food trucks, specialty drinks, vendors and live shows.

Must-visit LGBTIQ+ Neighborhood

Savannah's art-minded **Starland** (p140) hosts a Cheers Queers social event on the last Thursday of the month at Starland Park – $1 of every draft beer purchased is donated to the **Savannah Pride Center**. The center also sponsors a regular open-mic night at the nearby **Sentient Bean** (p141).

WHAT'S NEW

Named for a secret language used by marginalized groups, sultry **Bar Polari** *(barpolari.com)* in North Charleston is a cocktail bar for the LGBTIQ+ community. This intimate spot opened in 2024.

NEW AFRICA/SHUTTERSTOCK ©

SAVANNAH PRIDE CENTER

Advocacy and social hub for the LGBTIQ+ community. Scan this QR code to see wide-ranging programs and parties on its events page.

Resources

● **dudleys42ann.com** Long-running gay bar – but 'everybody's welcome' – in Charleston with drag bingo, trivia and open-mic nights. ● **visitsavannah.com** City tourism website with a few articles about LGBTIQ+ vacations in the city.

Health & Safe Travel

Charleston and Savannah are safe places to travel – just be aware of your surroundings at night. Check weather reports for hurricanes from late summer through fall.

OPEN CONTAINERS

If you are 21 years or older, you can legally – with some restrictions – stroll the Savannah Historic District with an open container of alcohol in a 16oz cup or can.

City Safety

Charleston and Savannah are considered safe cities with relatively low crime rates. That being said, be vigilant and avoid walking alone in areas where there aren't many people. According to the Savannah Police Department, the majority of crimes are car break-ins and petty theft. If you don't feel safe walking home in either city, it's fairly easy to hire a pedicab or Uber.

Ocean Safety

A red flag flying on the beach means no swimming, due to dangerous conditions.

Hurricanes

Tropical storms and hurricanes are likeliest June through November, with peak risk in August and September. Check weather reports just before your visit and during your trip. If a tropical storm warning or hurricane watch is issued, there's typically a 48-hour window before it makes landfall. Heed weather reports and on-the-ground information from local officials.

ALLIGATORS

American alligators lurk in many freshwater areas, particularly swamps and coastal marshes. Never approach or feed them, and avoid swimming in areas they're known to inhabit.

QUICK INFO

Travel insurance
Highly recommended to cover theft, loss and medical problems.

Rip currents
To escape an ocean rip, swim parallel to shore.

Car crashes
Abercorn St in Savannah sees frequent car crashes and pedestrian-related accidents.

Responsible Travel

Follow these tips to leave a lighter footprint, support local and have a positive impact on communities.

Etiquette Dos & Don'ts

Manners matter (p24) in this famously polite part of the country.

Taboo topics In general, keep thoughts on US politics to yourself – you never know who you might offend. Christian culture is overt; tread carefully with topics relating to religion.

Sensitivity about race These cities were centers of the trade in enslaved people, and places connected with that history should be treated with respect. Don't make insensitive jokes while touring plantations and museums.

Bicycling

Charleston has a **Lime** *(li.me/locations/charleston)* e-bike-share program with 200 bikes and numerous stations downtown and in surrounding neighborhoods. Some of the best cycling is on the sea islands near Charleston and Savannah.

AL MUNROE/SHUTTERSTOCK ©

OUR PICK

Forsyth Farmers' Market

Strolling the stalls at the Forsyth Park Farmers' Market is a fun way to chat with local farmers and producers while sampling Georgia's best produce.

What You Can Do

Opt for trains and buses rather than planes when possible. Where you can, take public transportation and explore on foot or bicycle rather than by car. Avoid overtourism by traveling outside of peak season (the peak is generally March to May and September to October). Visit major sites on weekdays rather than weekends.

Resources

- **southcarolinalowcountry.com** Lists farmers' markets in Beaufort, Bluffton and Hilton Head as well as nature tourism locations.
- **visitgullahgeechee.com** Shares Gullah-Geechee sites in South Carolina and Georgia.

ECO-FRIENDLY HILTON HEAD

The first eco-planned community in America, Hilton Head is home to island-crossing bike trails and nature preserves, and its Sea Turtle Patrol promotes a lights-out initiative protecting baby loggerheads.

Sea Turtles

Several species of sea turtle, including 250lb loggerheads, swim along the South Carolina and Georgia coasts. All are threatened or endangered according to the Environmental Species Act. During the May–October nesting season, hundreds of loggerheads return to the barrier-island beaches where they were born. Unfortunately, due to injury, disease and predators, only one in 4000 hatchlings survives to adulthood. The Sea Turtle Care Center at Charleston's Aquarium (p64) nurses those that are injured. To protect the hatchlings, don't use lights on the beach at night and don't disturb nests or turtles.

NATURE & ECO-TOURS

Scan the QR code above for a list of guided nature and eco-trips in the Charleston area.

For Savannah, scan the QR code below.

Climate Change & Travel

It's impossible to ignore the impact we have when traveling, and the importance of making changes where we can. Lonely Planet urges all travelers to engage with their travel carbon footprint. Many airlines and travel sites offer travelers the option of offsetting the impact of greenhouse gas emissions by contributing to climate-friendly initiatives around the world. We continue to offset the carbon footprint of all Lonely Planet staff travel while recognizing this is a mitigation more than a solution.

The **UN Carbon Offset Calculator** shows how flying impacts a household's emissions.

The **ICAO's carbon emissions calculator** allows visitors to analyse the CO_2 generated by point-to-point journeys.

Accessible Travel

Historic Districts

Most businesses in both cities comply with ADA regulations, and ramps and elevators are available at most multilevel sites. That said, uneven sidewalks, alleyways and cobblestone streets aren't great for wheelchairs. Historic house museums are typically not fully accessible for wheelchairs or scooters; check individual websites. Parks and riverfront areas are often wheelchair accessible.

Public Transportation

Managed by CARTA, fixed bus routes in Charleston are wheelchair accessible as buses have lifts to help wheelchair passengers to board. CAT buses in Savannah also kneel and have fold-out ramps.

Charleston-area Beaches: Accessibility

The following beaches and **Isle of Palms** (p93) have beach wheelchairs. Reservations may be required.

- **Folly Beach** (p94) Accessible beach walk and ramp.
- **Sullivan's Island** (p94) Accessible paths at Stations 18, 21 and 26.
- **Kiawah Beachwalker Park** (p94) Accessible boardwalk and ramp.

OUR PICK

With its iconic fountain, mossy live oaks and verdant lawns, 30-acre **Forsyth Park** (p118) is a Savannah showpiece. Broad sidewalks crisscross the park, and it's easy to admire the monuments, gardens and energy of this green space from a wheelchair. The newer of the park's two playgrounds (both are south of the fountain) is wheelchair accessible. Flower scents are a highlight at the tranquil **Fragrant Garden for the Blind** (9am-2pm Mon-Fri). Wheelchair-accessible picnic tables are nearby.

SHOPPING AT THE STACKS

A low-grade ramp climbs to the entrance of the **Stacks** *(thestacksbookstore.com)*, an inclusive, wheelchair-accessible bookstore that opened in 2023.

CHARLESTON: FORTS & FISH

For two interesting sites that are wheelchair-accessible and close to each other, visit Charleston's East Side, home to the South Carolina Aquarium (p64) and the Fort Sumter Visitor Education Center at Liberty Square (p59).

Resources

- **visitsavannah.com/savannahs-accessibility**
- **charlestoncvb.com/travel-support/accessibility/**

Nuts & Bolts

Opening Hours

Opening hours vary throughout the year. Below are high-season opening hours; hours often get shorter in the shoulder and low seasons.

Banks 9am to 5pm Monday to Friday

Cafes 7am to 7pm

Bars and clubs 5pm to 2am

Shops 10am to 6pm

QUICK INFO

Time zone
Eastern Standard Time (GMT/UTC minus five hours)

Emergency number
911

City of Charleston population 159,333

City of Savannah population 147,748

ELECTRICITY

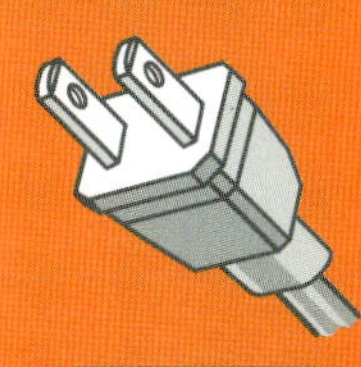

Type A 120V/60Hz

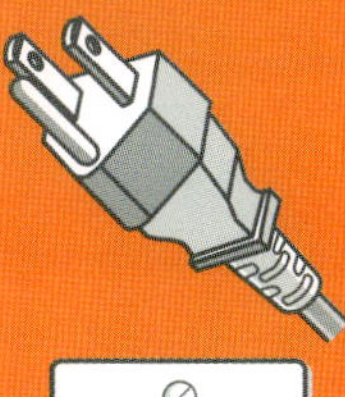

Type B 120V/60Hz

Public Holidays

Major holidays may mean many businesses are closed, or they may attract crowds, making dining and accommodations reservations difficult.

New Year's Day January 1

Martin Luther King Jr Day Third Monday in January

Presidents' Day Third Monday in February

St Patrick's Day March 17

Easter March/April

Memorial Day Last Monday in May

Juneteenth Mid-June, Georgia only

Independence Day July 4

Labor Day First Monday in September

Thanksgiving Fourth Thursday in November

Christmas Day December 25

New Year's Eve December 31

Toilets

Public restrooms can be hard to find in both cities. Your best bets in Charleston are the Charleston Visitor Center, the Fort Sumter Visitor Education Center at Liberty Sq and the City Market. City Hall on Broad St is your best option in the South of Broad area. In Savannah you'll find restrooms at Ellis Sq, the Bryan and Liberty St parking garages, the visitor center on MLK Blvd and the River Street Visitor Information Center.

Index

Sights p000 Map pages **p000**

See also separate subindexes for:
Eating p174
Drinking p175
Shopping p175

Eating

Drinking

Shopping

Send Us Your Feedback

We love to hear from travellers – your comments help make our books better. We read every word, and we guarantee that your feedback goes straight to the authors. Visit lonelyplanet.com/contact to submit your updates and suggestions.

Note: We may edit, reproduce and incorporate your comments in Lonely Planet products such as guidebooks, websites and digital products, so let us know if you are happy to have your name acknowledged. For a copy of our privacy policy visit lonelyplanet.com/legal.

Acknowledgements

Cover photograph:
Savannah (p113). Sean Pavone/ Shutterstock ©

Back photograph:
Forsyth Park (p118). Jon Lovette/ Getty Images ©

THIS BOOK

Destination Editors
Caroline Trefler
Amy Balfour

Cartographer
Eve Kelly

Production Editor
Robin Yule

Book Designer
Dermot Hegarty

Coordinating Editor
Sarah Bailey

Cover Researcher
Gwen Cotter

Thanks to
James Appleton, Liana Cafolla, Karen Henderson, Alison Killilea

Paper in this book is certified against the Forest Stewardship Council™ standards. FSC™ promotes environmentally responsible, socially beneficial and economically viable management of the world's forests.

Published by Lonely Planet Global Limited
CRN 554153
3rd edition – Aug 2025
ISBN 978 1 83758 483 3

10 9 8 7 6 5 4 3 2 1
Printed in China